GAMES FOR LE...

DATE			

Also by Peggy Kaye

GAMES FOR MATH

GAMES FOR READING

GAGES FOR LEARNING

TEN MINUTES A DAY TO HELP
YOUR CHILD DO WELL IN SCHOOL

from Kindergarten to Third Grade

WRITTEN BY **Peggy Kaye**

WITH ILLUSTRATIONS
BY THE AUTHOR

THE NOONDAY PRESS
FARRAR STRAUS GIROUX
NEW YORK

Published simultaneously in Canada by HarperCollins*CanadaLtd*
Printed in the United States of America
This edition first published by The Noonday Press, 1991

Library of Congress Cataloging-in-Publication Data
Kaye, Peggy.
    Games for learning : ten minutes a day to help your child do well
in school—from kindergarten to third grade / written by Peggy Kaye
; with illustrations by the author. — 1st ed.
        p. cm.
    1. Educational games.   2. Education, Primary—Activity programs.
3. Kindergarten—Activity programs.   4. Education—Parent
participation.   I. Title.
LB1029.G3K387 1991   372.13'078—dc20   90-28507   CIP

CONTENTS

PART TWO: READ AND WRITE

Chapter 3: Word Power

Chapter 4: Sounds Abound

Chapter 5: Reading and Meaning

Chapter 9: Size and Shape

Chapter 10: Multiplication and Division

PART FOUR: OTHER SUBJECTS

Chapter 11: Science

Chapter 12: Social Studies

APPENDICES

ACKNOWLEDGMENTS

All the games in this book, and the many failed games that won't ever appear in any book, were tested by a crew of very helpful children, my students. I thank them for their willingness to play and their thoroughly honest opinions. Thanks also to Sara Bershtel for her taste and good sense, her colleagues at Farrar, Straus and Giroux, and, as always, Paul Berman.

INTRODUCTION

Games for Learning is a collection of eighty-four games that parents can play with children. The games are very simple, and each one takes a mere ten minutes or less from start to finish. You can play them anywhere—at the dinner table, on the bus, in the laundromat. All you need is ten minutes and a willingness to have fun. But these particular games have the special advantage of being, from an educational point of view, extremely useful. They will help your child do better in school.

Children have to master a great number of skills in the early grades. The statistically average child entering kindergarten has some working knowledge of the alphabet and can count from one to fourteen. That same child, by the end of third grade, should be able to read with considerable fluency, spell easily, write stories and reports, add, subtract, multiply, and divide with precision, know a little about science, history, and geography too. A great deal to learn! Of course, the normal school program will teach all these topics. But as I have discovered in many years of teaching, both in the classroom and tutoring children one-to-one, game-playing can be a perfect aid.

Games can help a child learn and practice almost every skill that school requires. And games can do this in a wonderfully effective manner. For when a child sits down to play a well-designed and interesting game, the child relaxes and concentrates at the same time—relaxes because the game is entertaining, and concentrates because the game is challenging. A child who simultaneously relaxes and concentrates is in a perfect frame of mind for learning.

Time and again, individual children have given me renewed proof of the usefulness of games. Sam, for instance, was a first-grader who needed to review addition. He couldn't sit still, though. That was a problem. I handed him math worksheets, but he couldn't even look at them. So we played games. Games glued him to his seat. We rolled dice on the table. He was eager and alert; yet in figuring out the dice totals, we were reviewing the same pesky arithmetic problems that he couldn't tolerate on the worksheet. Lola, on the other hand, was a superior math student. She loved any kind of math lesson. Her delight increased tenfold, however, when lessons involved tossing coins on a paper number target or playing with a deck of cards.

Joyce—to take another example—was a second-grader who had trouble sounding out words from the way they're spelled, and this inability frustrated her. To help her, we played games that sharpened her perception of sounds. She enjoyed herself. She relaxed. She concentrated—and her ability to sound out words improved. Billy was a precocious kindergartener who was itching to read. He was too young for formal lessons. But there were games to play, and the games opened a window on words for him. Susan needed help with handwriting. Pooh-like, her letters wobbled. Games came to the rescue.

Games are a good way for parents to get involved in their children's education, and parental involvement is always a good idea. There has been a lot of research showing that a helpful parent can play a crucial role in a child's school performance. Comparisons with other countries—Japan, for instance, where parents actively involve themselves in the educational process—confirm the usefulness of parent participation. This helpfulness is only logical. Parents are the most important adults in any child's life. When you, the parent, are concerned, interested, and involved in learning, you send a powerful message to your child about education. You inspire the child. And you can help teach specific skills.

How far parents should go in teaching is a question, naturally. Some parents set out to teach the "three R's" in a comprehensive curriculum. Usually that's too ambitious a goal. Other parents become drillmasters armed with flash cards and workbooks. That, too, can be a bad idea. What, then, should parents do? Parents should help in an entertaining and affectionate way. The moments of interaction should be enjoyable. That is the reason for playing educationally useful games. Of course, parents are busy and may not have hours at their disposal. But hours aren't necessary. A few minutes a day with the right game will still sharpen a child's skills.

Games for Learning follows the school curriculum. All major topics for kindergarteners through third-graders are included in one game or another. In Part One: Think About It, you'll find games that enhance a child's ability to gather information with his eyes and ears. Accurate perception is a central pillar of all learning. Other games in the first part help a child write letters and numbers with ease, to improve handwriting. You'll find an entire chapter of logic games, very useful for sharpening the intellect.

The second part is called Read and Write. Each of the chapters in this part takes up a different aspect of reading and writing: learning new words, sounding them out, reading with understanding, and writing stories, both true and make-believe.

Part Three: Counting on Math will give you and your child a chance to play with counting, addition, subtraction, multiplication, division, geometry, measurement, and a bit of number theory.

Part Four: Other Subjects offers science and social studies games. These games promote intellectual curiosity and creative thinking.

How should you choose which games to play? Some parents may want to read the book from cover to cover, looking for games in a systematic manner. Flipping through the pages at random is also a perfectly satisfactory method. Some parents will stick to math games and keep away from the logic and social studies games, or vice versa. Your own preference is a good guide. A well-chosen game will appeal to you as well as your child. If you yourself aren't amused, browse through for another game.

How will you know what is right for your child? Each game is assigned a suggested grade level, which should help you decide. But don't be too strict about grade levels. Often it's a good idea for third-graders to play games that are suggested for the first or second grade. Easier games give older children a chance to review, which is always valuable. Even professional baseball players benefit from a daily round of catch. Pushing a child into playing games that are above his head is another matter, however—soon you'll hear, "This is boring." When children complain of boredom, often they are really saying, "This is too hard. Give me something easier so I can relax and enjoy myself." Whatever game you select, in ten minutes you'll know if you've hit on a good choice. Every game isn't for everyone. If either you or your child doesn't like a game, then pick again. The right game will turn up soon enough.

You may want to play a special game over and over, or you may want to select a new game every day. You may decide to play games during daily car rides. You may limit play to rainy Sundays. There are no set rules or regulations about when to play. The more you play, however, the more you help your child. A game a day— ten minutes a day—over the course of a school year is a playful but successful way to help your child grow academically. Each game sharpens a particular skill, and day by day these skills add up. All children can benefit from playing: those who are doing well in school, and those who need improvement. Even children with serious learning difficulties can benefit from the games—though, of course, if your child has serious academic trouble you should probably ask a teacher for advice.

Game-playing does carry with it the problem of competition. Children love competitive games. But they hate losing and don't always take their defeats in good grace. Why is winning so vital to children? First and foremost: winning is fun, losing is not. It's also true that children equate winning with skill rather than luck, no matter what kind of game is played. They believe that losing reflects on their own ability, which makes losing painful to accept. Children especially want to show off their abilities to Mom and Dad, as is only natural. Thus, your child may find it particularly difficult to make mistakes or do badly while playing with you.

There are three ways to get around this problem. You can avoid competitive games altogether. Many games in this book are decidedly noncompetitive but still lots of fun to play. Second, you can let your child win. This keeps the child happy and eager to play some more. Personally, I make frequent use of this ancient child-management tactic. Third, you can deal with your child's unhappiness directly when he does lose a game. Living is losing, at least some of the time. It's a dismal lesson, but you'll have to teach it sooner or later, and a ten-minute game is a relatively painless way to begin. A sympathetic attitude can help. Humor helps too. Tell your child, "It's okay to make mistakes. After all, you aren't a computer—thank goodness. What would I give a computer for dessert tonight?" As long as you keep the game-playing light and fun, your child will be fine.

Fun is the operative word. Learning at home with games should be a pleasure. Your child should enjoy it, and so should you. Possibly the deepest lesson these games should teach is that concentration and intellectual challenge can be immensely enjoyable. The child who learns that will benefit forever.

PART ONE
THINK ABOUT IT

chapter 1

The Hand, the Ear, the Eye

Jane, a second-grader, was having a miserable time in school. She had trouble coping with every academic subject. Nothing was going right. Her classroom teacher sent her to me for private tutoring. After a month of one-to-one sessions, the classroom teacher reported a big improvement in Jane's work at school. Her parents reported a change in her mood at home. Things were suddenly going nicely. Jane's mother asked me, "Exactly what is your program with Jane? She says you just play games."

Jane and I did play a lot of games. At first glance, these games had nothing to do with reading, writing, or math. Instead, the games merely sharpened Jane's skills with her hand, her ears, and her eyes. But hand games, ear games, and eye games were exactly what she needed.

What are hand games? These are games that helped Jane develop better muscle control over her hands and fingers. She needed precise finger control in order to write numbers and letters with ease. Without this control, learning to write was agony for her.

What are ear games? Some ear games helped Jane hear subtle differences between similar sounds: for instance, the difference between *p* and *b*. Other games helped her develop a memory for sounds. As her memory for sounds increased, she had an easier time recalling all the different pronunciations of the twenty-six letters in our alphabet. Jane needed a good memory for sounds during math time too. Mastering the addition, subtraction, multiplication, and division tables is hard work. The task is less daunting, though, for children with good auditory memories. They don't need to work out each problem. Instead, quick recall allows them to link the words *six plus five* and the words *equals eleven* with no more effort than it takes to remember the names of the numbers.

What are eye games? Jane and I played three different types of eye games. First, we played games to help Jane register the tiny visual differences between letters like *b* and *d* and words like *want* and *went*. A second kind of eye game helped her remember things she saw. A strong visual memory is crucial for success in reading: by the end of third grade, Jane would need to have instant visual recall of more than a thousand words in order to keep up with her schoolwork. Finally, we played games that helped Jane organize and analyze visual information. Which two of these five shapes are identical?

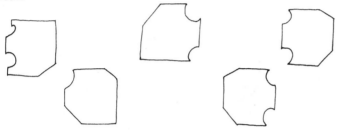

To find out, you must make a visual analysis of the shapes. You must analyze notches, angles, directions, sizes, and sides. Children who can make such shrewd visual judgments tend to be good math students.

You'll find many of Jane's favorite games in this chapter. DRAWN TO ORDER, BEADED WRITING, and TRIPLE LETTERS are hand games. These games make handwriting fun for beginners as well as for more advanced students who could use extra help. Next come games for the ear: SOUND DETECTIVE and SOUND MEM-ORIES. Finally come games for the eye: CLOSE YOUR EYES, FLASH LOOKS, MATCHING NUMBERS, and FARMER AND HIS CROPS. Pick any of these games, read the instructions, gather the materials you need (never more than a pencil, crayons or colored pencils, and paper), and spend ten minutes or less playing. Your child will gradually become a little more accurate with his hands, his ears, and his eyes. The skills may not seem related to academic work. But without these skills, academic success can be hopelessly difficult.

DRAWN TO ORDER

GRADES

kindergarten and first

MATERIALS

paper
crayons or colored pencils

Julia was a precocious first-grader. She had taught herself to read in kindergarten. She was a whiz with numbers. For Julia, school was a fine place where work was fun and easy—until she started handwriting lessons. She couldn't control her hands. Her letters and numbers were squiggly things, typical of many younger children but hateful to an achiever and perfectionist like Julia. During one handwriting lesson she burst into frustrated tears. "I can't make my fingers work!" she cried.

What could help Julia's fingers work? More writing would only mean more frustration. So instead I introduced a drawing game called DRAWN TO ORDER.

I picked a bright green crayon and drew a free-flowing shape in the middle of a blank sheet of paper.

I told Julia to pick a color and use it to surround my shape with a slightly larger echo of the original. She added a line of lemon yellow.

4

Now it was my turn to enlarge matters in the color of my choice: deep green.

"Ah," Julia said as she started drawing a purple line, "this is getting pretty."

We continued drawing larger and larger shapes until one of us hit the edge of the paper.

Julia enjoyed DRAWN TO ORDER. That was lucky. She needed to make many such drawings to develop good command over her fingers. With every drawing, Julia forced her hands to obey more and more. She had to exercise control or else our drawings would lose their lovely rippling effect. Unlike writing letters or numbers, however, if her fingers didn't "work" perfectly nothing was ruined. An overly large ripple or an overlapped line here and there didn't distract from the beauty of our pictures.

BEADED WRITING

GRADES

first and second

MATERIALS

paper
pencil
crayons or colored pencils

BEADED WRITING is an unusual but effective way to help your child's penmanship. Here's how to make a beaded letter. Start by writing a letter in a light pencil stroke:

Then go back over the letter, transforming the line to tiny circular beads:

Finally, take crayons or colored pencils and fill in each circle. You can use as many different colors as you like. When you finish your first letter, bead a second. Bead a word. Bead a sentence. Bead numbers too.

Your child might like to bead birthday cards, welcome-home banners, and DO NOT ENTER MY ROOM! signs. The more beading you do today, tomorrow, next week, and again next month, the more practice your child gets correctly forming his p's and q's. With twenty-six uppercase and twenty-six lowercase letters to learn, children need all the practice they can get.

TRIPLE LETTERS

GRADES

first and second

MATERIALS

paper
colored pencils

Andrea was bored with handwriting lessons. She did want to form her letters correctly and to make her papers look nice, but she didn't want to practice letter after letter after letter. Fortunately, there are other ways to help a child with penmanship aside from endlessly writing letters in the same old way. TRIPLE LETTERS—a colorful, playful alternative—rescued Andrea from boredom.

To begin, I told Andrea to select three different pencils from my colored pencil collection. She grabbed orange, red, and blue. Now she needed words to write with those pencils. Something silly. Something weird. I made three suggestions: *green squirts, fuzzy eggs*, or *lemon spiders*. She liked *fuzzy eggs* best. Colors in hand, slogan selected, Andrea was ready to write in triplicate. She began by making the neatest *f* she could with her red pencil.

Next she repeated the *f* in blue.

Then she drew a third *f* in orange.

After she'd tripled the *f*, she went on writing, until a trio of *fuzzy eggs* appeared.

fuzzy eggs

Andrea was proud of herself. She had worked hard. She had written her letters with care. And she wasn't bored. What did I do while Andrea worked? I wrote—in proper TRIPLE LETTERS form—*chimpanzee fleas*. When we were both finished, we compared our papers, admired our handiwork, and laughed at the silly words.

If you want to try TRIPLE LETTERS at your house, all you need are colored pencils, paper, and a few strange expressions. Here's a list to get you going:

sleepy shoes
rubber lollipop
snake milk shake
jelly ink
racing radios
pizza bubble gum
skating telephones
cotton dice
zipper vipers
beastly buttons

SOUND DETECTIVE

It's a cold night outside. Inside, it's quiet—the quiet that comes before a game of SOUND DETECTIVE. Your child is sitting with eyes closed while you skulk around the room. Silently you stand by the bureau; then you say, "Beep bong," or "Fitz tsk," or any other silly sounds that suit your mood. Your child, with closed eyes, tries to point his finger at you. When he believes he's pointing to the correct spot, he opens his eyes and checks out his SOUND DETECTIVE skills. Did he hunt you down? What a detective!

Next it's your turn to close your eyes and your child's turn to "beep" or "bong" from one or another corner of the room. You'll discover how intensely you must listen to track your child accurately. Listening intensely is the point of the game.

Why is this important? Beginning readers need to hear in a more precise way than they've ever heard before. They have to hear the difference between *d* and *t*. They have to remember what sound goes with *f* and the several sounds that go with *a*. In order to remember and distinguish letter sounds, a child needs to be acutely sensitive to the tiniest variation in sound. SOUND DETECTIVE helps a child develop sharp ears. As the child struggles to seek out your exact location, not with his eyes but with his ears, little sounds—a "fitz," a "tsk"—are his only clues. Play the game now and then for a few weeks and you may notice the increased speed and accuracy with which your child follows the smallest sound you make. Sharp ears lead to sharper reading, and that's the great payoff for your "cheeps" and "chirps."

*G*eorge was in first grade and having trouble learning to read. He couldn't remember what sounds went with which letters. Did *f* make the sound *sssss*? Did *m* make the sound *eh*? George couldn't recollect. For the moment, his memory failures were affecting only his work in reading. Soon, though, he'd have to memorize more than two hundred addition and subtraction facts. He'd have to hear the words *three plus five* and respond immediately with *eight*. He needed to develop a stronger memory: otherwise his problems were going to get worse.

Developing a stronger memory isn't much different than developing any other skill. It takes practice. If you get a child to exercise his memory and if you do it every day a little more, the child's ability to remember will increase. Think of batting practice. If your child goes out on the field every day, then slowly but surely the bat and ball will connect more often.

For George, and all the other children in my acquaintance, games are the best way to practice. George and I played SOUND MEMORIES more than any other memory game. Why? Because it was quick, easy, fun, and effective.

At the beginning of our first tutoring session, I recited a silly sentence: *A giraffe ate my cornflakes this morning.* George repeated the sentence a couple of times. Then we went on to other work. Later in the hour, however, I turned to George and asked him to repeat the day's sentence. Sometimes he recalled it easily. Other times he wrinkled his face, pounded his fist, and said, "It was something about cornflakes, but I can't remember."

I gave him hints. "A giraffe . . ." I said. If that didn't do it, I added, ". . . ate my cornflakes. . . ." If that didn't work, I finished the sentence, ". . . this morning." Then I reassured him: "SOUND MEMORIES is supposed to be hard. If it were easy to remember the words, the game would be pretty boring."

Of course, you don't want the game to get *too* hard for your child. You can, and should, control the degree of difficulty. Short, simple sentences—*Stick a flower in your toenail*—are easier to recall than long, complicated ones—*A three-hundred-pound roller*

SOUND MEMORIES

GRADES

kindergarten and first

The Hand, the Ear, the Eye

skate crashed into the Tyrannosaurus rex who invaded New York last week. (It's a good idea to have your child repeat any sentence you choose two or three times; while giggling over the words, he is committing the sentence to memory.) Time is another variable. When George was a newcomer to SOUND MEMORIES, I waited just five minutes before asking him to recall the words. As he got better at the game, I let longer intervals go by. Eventually, I waited until the end of a tutoring session—a whole hour—before testing his memory.

When should you play this game? You can give your child a SOUND MEMORIES sentence as he begins his soup and see if he remembers it before he starts his sandwich. You can say a sentence at the start of a short car trip and see if the child remembers it when you reach your destination. Or propose a sentence before your child steps into a bath and ask him to recollect it when his hair is dry. If you have two children of different ages, you can give each one their own sentence. It's easy to adjust levels so the younger child has as good a chance of remembering as his older sibling.

But remember: SOUND MEMORIES is supposed to be amusing. If you make the game a dreary task, you will make your child anxious, and anxiety will defeat your purpose.

Does your child remember what he sees? Children who have a strong memory for the way things look learn to read new words easily. These children see the word *farm* once or twice and afterward can read it automatically. They enjoy the same advantage in mathematics. They merely glance at the equation $4 + 8 = 13$ and immediately SEE that something is wrong.

How can you strengthen your child's visual memory? CLOSE YOUR EYES is a simple way. This game is so speedy you can play it during TV commercials. Begin by telling your child to take a good look at you. Then have him close his eyes. While his eyes are closed, ask him what color shirt you're wearing. Can he say? If not, give him a few extra seconds to study you again, then tell him to close his eyes once more. Now ask if your hands are resting at your sides or on your lap. Can he say? Can he picture you accurately in his mind? Does he remember what he sees?

How about you? How good are you at this game? Your child surely deserves a chance to test Mom or Dad. A question or two for your child, a question or two for you, and the commercials will be over.

GRADES

kindergarten and first

FLASH LOOKS

GRADES

kindergarten, first, and second

MATERIALS

paper
pencil

Manuel had trouble distinguishing subtle differences in the appearance of letters and words. He confused *b* and *d*, turning *big* into *dig*. He confused *m* and *w*, turning *met* into *wet*. He confused *on* and *no*, *was* and *saw*, *stop* and *spot*. These are common errors with beginning readers, but troublesome nevertheless. In this case, the main trouble was Manuel's frustration over his frequent mix-ups. He believed such mistakes were proof positive that he would *never* learn to read. Manuel's fears were unfounded. Still, he had to master the hard-to-distinguish letters and words before his reading could improve and he could feel better about himself. FLASH LOOKS—a visual game involving no words whatsoever—developed Manuel's ability to distinguish between subtle visual differences and, in time, improved his reading.

To prepare the game, I took a piece of typing paper and tore it into about five strips.

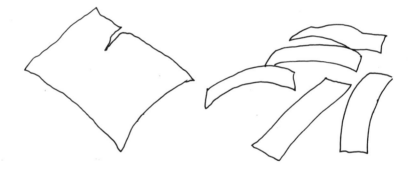

Next I drew a line across the middle of one strip. On both sides of the line I drew a simple design. Sometimes the designs were the same.

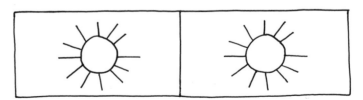

Sometimes they were different.

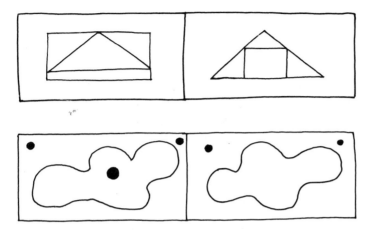

While drawing, I was careful to keep the paper out of Manuel's sight. When I finished working, I showed him the designs. He never got FLASH LOOKS, however, for more than a few seconds. When time was up, Manuel had to declare if the designs were the same or different. Big differences were easy.

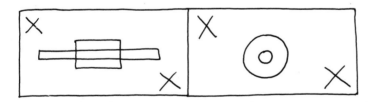

Minuscule differences gave him more trouble.

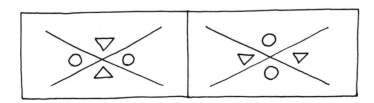

I always tried to give Manuel a range of FLASH LOOKS from easy to hard. The game ended when he looked at the last strip.

FLASH LOOKS took less than two minutes to play. This was one of its attractions. Manuel's tutoring sessions lasted an hour. Sixty minutes is a long time for a second-grader to concentrate on academic work. He needed to take a break now and then. What to do during the break? We played FLASH LOOKS. That way, Manuel got his break—and the tutoring wasn't interrupted.

Here is a visual puzzle. You see before you two squares with sides numbered 1 through 8. Both squares contain parts of circles. If you place the two squares together correctly, you will make two perfect circles. The squares can be turned any which way. There is only one correct solution. Which sides go together?

GRADES

first and second

MATERIALS

paper
pencil

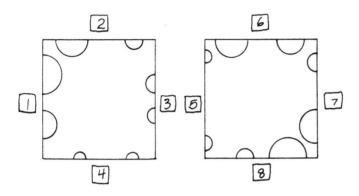

If you picked sides 2 and 7, you have excellent ability to analyze visual information.

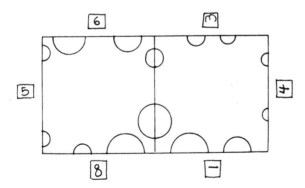

You are, in educational terms, a strong spatial thinker, someone who is good at analyzing visual information. Research shows that children who are strong spatial thinkers tend to do well in mathematics.

The next two games help develop children's spatial thinking. The easiest of them is MATCHING NUMBERS. To play, take a blank sheet of paper and write the numbers 1 through 10 randomly all over the page. When you're done writing this first set, write a second set—again, 1 through 10. Place this duplicate set randomly around the page as well. When you're finished, the page will look something like this:

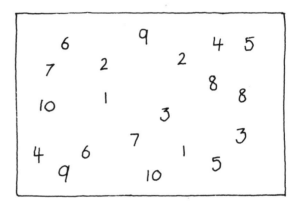

Your child's job is to draw lines connecting number twins. He must draw a line from 1 to 1. He must draw a line from 2 to 2. He must keep drawing lines until every number is linked up.

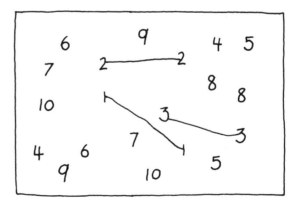

But—he must not cross any lines. If a player crosses a line while linking numbers, the game is lost. Here is a completed winning game board:

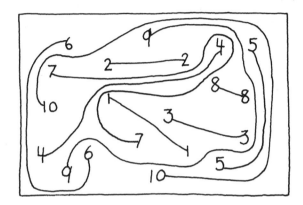

To win at MATCHING NUMBERS, your child has to analyze every line. He must be convinced that the line linking 5 to 5 won't interfere later on with a line linking 8 to 8. By the time the child links 9 to 9 and 10 to 10, the maze of lines gets pretty complicated. Still, in my experience, every MATCHING NUMBERS board can be a winning board.

When your child is ready for a greater challenge, increase the range of numbers. Instead of 1 through 10, try working with 1 through 20, or 1 through 30. Matching so many numbers is a big accomplishment for any child.

FARMER AND HIS CROPS

FARMER AND HIS CROPS is similar to MATCHING NUMBERS, although a bit more difficult. Here's a sample game board:

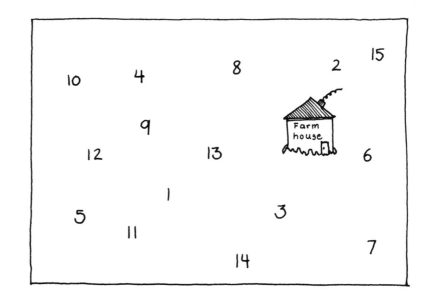

It shows the farmer's house and his fifteen crops—each crop represented by a number. Time has come for the farmer to gather his crops. You must help him. You must draw a path from the farmer's house to each of his crops and back to the house again. There are two rules. First: you must gather the crops in numerical order. You go from crop 1 to crop 2 to crop 3 and so on until you finish harvesting and return to the farmer's house. Second rule:

you must not cross any lines. If you can gather all fifteen crops in numerical order and get back to the farmhouse without crossing any lines, you win. Bonanza! Here's a winning board:

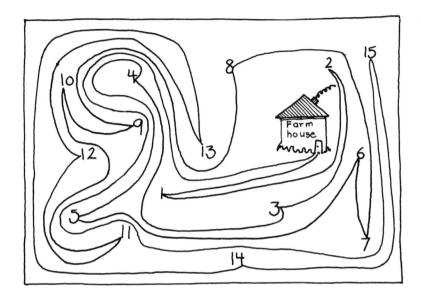

When you make your own board, the house can go anywhere you like, and the same with the crops. You might start with ten crops, and go up to fifteen later on. When the child gets good at the game, add more and more. Each time you play, you can create a new board and a new challenge for your child. Let your child make a board for you too. Reaping what was sown is not easy business—as you'll see.

chapter 2

Logical Thinking

I showed Laura, age five, a vase filled with half a dozen tulips and three roses. I asked her a variety of questions about the flowers.

"Laura," I began, "can you count how many flowers are in the vase?"

"Yes. One, two, three, four, five, six, seven, eight, nine. Nine flowers."

"That's right. You counted beautifully," I said. "Now, can you tell me if there are more tulips or more roses?"

Laura glanced at the vase and answered, "More tulips."

I asked, "Are there more tulips or more flowers?"

Laura looked at the vase again and answered, "More tulips."

A strange answer. Perhaps Laura hadn't understood my question. I took a different approach.

"Can you point to all the tulips?" I asked.

"Yes," she said, and pointed to each one.

"Can you point to all the flowers?" I asked.

"Yes," she said, and pointed to all nine flowers.

"Are there more tulips or more flowers?" I asked again.

Laura answered, "There are more tulips."

"Why do you think so?" I asked.

"Because there are six tulips and only three of the others."

I tried another tactic. "Are all the tulips flowers?" I asked.

"Yes," she answered.

"Are all the roses flowers?" I asked.

"Yes," she answered.

"So both the tulips *and* the roses are flowers?" I asked.

"Yes," she answered.

"Do you like the flowers?"

"Sure," she answered.

"Would you like to take as many as you can home with you?" I asked.

"Yes," she answered.

"Well, then, you can take all the flowers or you can take all the tulips. Which would you rather?" I asked.

"I want all the tulips because that's more," Laura replied.

No matter how I phrased the question, Laura didn't get it. Why? Laura understood the relationship between tulips and roses. But she didn't have the logical reasoning to understand the relationship between tulips and flowers. The Swiss psychologist Jean Piaget was the first to use flowers as a way of demonstrating that young children reason differently than adults. That's *all* young children— no exceptions, not even young Albert Einstein. Piaget also proved that adults cannot teach children to reason more logically. It's like trying to make a child grow faster than his genetic makeup determines. It can't be done. You can, however, help your child grow as strong as possible at his own pace. You can provide good food, exercise, fresh air and sunlight. It is much the same when dealing with your child's mental development. Logical thinking develops in its own time in all children. You can't accelerate the process. You can, however, provide experiences that promote the strongest possible growth in logical thinking. And the stronger a child's logical abilities, the better prepared he'll be for all academic work.

That's the point of the six games in this chapter. THE CLUB GAME and STRING ALONG help children form logical groups and subgroups. ALIKE/UNALIKE and MR. YUM'S COOKIES help children organize information in a logical manner. FIX IT and PATTERN GRIDS help children create and analyze eminently logical visual patterns. Play these games again and again. Clearly, it's the logical thing to do.

THE CLUB GAME

For a young child, crucial ideas—ideas about numbers, for instance—only become clear when the child can form logical groups. A young child will look at five pencils, five cookies, five cups and won't see anything in common in this odd collection. As his logical thinking grows, he'll see a commonality: five, five, five. The child can now classify all the objects together on the basis of number. He'll avoid all the other aspects of pencils, cookies, and cups. Logic lets him focus on the numerical way to classify groups. This is a giant intellectual step. Before the child can take this step, however, he must have lots of experiences describing and forming all kinds of logical groups.

THE CLUB GAME gives children the opportunity to create such groups. The game is valuable for all children, and for those who have trouble with this kind of thinking, it is invaluable. In the case of Carolyn, I began almost every work session by playing a round or two of THE CLUB GAME.

Peggy: I'm thinking of a club. It's a club of animals. In fact, only *wild* animals can belong. Let's see if we can list seven creatures that belong in the club. Can you think of any wild animals?

Carolyn: How about lions?

Peggy: An excellent animal. Now I'm thinking of something more spotty than a lion. Can you guess what it is?

Carolyn: Is it a tiger?

Peggy: Tiger is a good answer. But I'm thinking of a different animal. I'm thinking of leopards. Lions, tigers, and leopards—we already have three animals in our club. We only need four more.

Carolyn: Bears are wild.

Peggy: They sure are. Can you think of anything else?

Carolyn: I'm stuck.

Peggy: I know a club member who's huge and has a long trunk.

Carolyn: An elephant!

Peggy: Right. Just two more.

Carolyn: Are snakes wild animals?

Peggy: Snakes are definitely wild. Which kind do you mean?

Carolyn: Rattlesnakes.

Peggy: Very wild. Good going, Carolyn, we just need one more animal to complete our list.

Carolyn: I'm trying to think of animals at the zoo.

Peggy: That's a good idea. What comes to mind?

Carolyn: I'm trying to think. Monkeys! Oh, that's no good; monkeys can be tame.

Peggy: Some monkeys are tame, like the ones that go around with organ-grinders, but others aren't. If you don't want to include monkeys, you can pick another animal. Can you think of something like a monkey, only bigger and wilder?

Carolyn: How about gorillas? They're really wild!

Peggy: Congratulations to us! Our list is full.

Carolyn used sophisticated thinking while forming her club. It takes logical reasoning to group lions, rattlesnakes, and gorillas together while excluding all sorts of other animals like kittens and hamsters.

You can help your child think just as logically by playing THE CLUB GAME. Here's a list of clubs you can use to get started:

> nine things that need electricity
> twelve foods fit for a monster
> five things with four wheels
> ten musical instruments
> seven things you only wear in the winter
> fifteen delicious desserts
> ten flying things (no birds allowed)

STRING ALONG

Joe and I played many rounds of THE CLUB GAME. Joe became an expert at it. Too expert perhaps, because over time the game lost its punch. Joe and I didn't stop playing category games, however. I just switched from THE CLUB GAME to STRING ALONG. The basic concept of the two games is the same, but STRING ALONG is a little tougher to tackle.

"Joe," I said at the beginning of our first game, "I want you to name something blue."

"That's easy," he said. "A crayon is blue."

"Good," I said. "This time name something blue and soft."

Joe replied, "My sweater. It's blue and soft."

"Excellent," I said. "Now, can you name something blue and soft and *not* clothing?"

"Uh-oh," Joe said. "This is getting hard. I have to think."

Yes indeed, he had to think, and that was the point of the game. After a few moments' consideration, Joe declared, "A blue flower. Flowers can be blue. Flowers are soft. Flowers aren't clothes."

"Good work!" I exclaimed. "Want to try again?"

"Okay, let's go," he said.

For his next logical workout, Joe had to name a game (big category). Then, a game you play for points (subcategory). Then a game for points that you play with a ball (subcategory of a subcategory). Finally, a game for points that you play with a ball but in which you don't use your hands (subcategory of a subcategory of a subcategory—whew!). What could that be? Soccer!

Logicians and mathematicians like to show this kind of grouping with a Venn diagram.

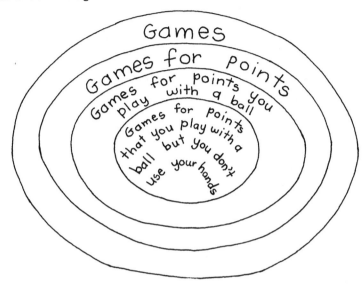

In recent years, Venn diagrams have made their way into the upper grades of elementary-school math programs. Why? Because thinking logically about categories and subcategories helps children with math. It helps children understand science and technology too. Computer programming, for instance, requires this kind of thinking.

Joe wasn't ready for diagrams. He wasn't about to program computers, either. But he was ready for STRING ALONG.

ALIKE/UNALIKE

first, second, and third

One spring day, I heard a small child ask his mother: "How come you take flowers home from the store and I can't take them home from the park?"

I understood the child's confusion. In his mind, if it's wrong to take flowers from the park it must be wrong to take them from the florist. For a preschooler, it may be hard to grasp that some flowers go home and other flowers do not. Young children think in rigid ways. The older the child, the more subtle the thinking becomes—and yet a certain rigidity may remain. This isn't always obvious. But get into certain arguments, even with a teenager, and the lack of flexibility is painfully obvious.

A simple game called ALIKE/UNALIKE can help children to think in a less rigid manner. I played it often with Kate. She liked the game because it was fun to play, and I liked it because the game helped her learn.

I started by naming two objects: *sweater* and *blanket*. Then Kate had to think of a way in which a sweater and a blanket are alike and a way in which they're unalike.

Kate didn't hesitate: "A sweater is like a blanket because they both keep you warm. A sweater isn't like a blanket because you wear a sweater and you don't wear a blanket."

"Wow, Kate, that was easy for you. I'm impressed. The next ALIKE/UNALIKE I give you will have to be harder. First, though, you can give me one. You can pick any two things in the universe and I'll have to say how they're alike and how they're unalike."

Kate wanted to give me a hard time, and she did, by making her ALIKE/UNALIKE challenge a chicken and a bathing suit.

"What could these two things have in common?" I wondered aloud. "Chickens are alive, but bathing suits aren't. There's the unalike part. Chickens have feathers. Are there feathered bathing suits? No, I guess not, or at least I hope not. Chickens are colorful. That's it! Chickens are colorful and so are bathing suits. That's how they're alike. You gave me a tough one, but I got it. Now here's a toughie for you: bicycles and pencils."

"You write with pencils and you don't write with bicycles. That's the unalike part," said Kate.

"Good, but how are they alike?" I asked.

"I can't think of a way. I guess I lose."

"No, you can't lose in this game. We'll come up with something. How about describing a bicycle. That might help."

"A bicycle has wheels," Kate said.

"Do pencils have wheels?" I asked.

"No," she answered. "Bicycles have seats."

"Do pencils have seats?" I asked.

"No," she said.

Kate seemed stumped, so I asked a leading question.

"What do bicycles do?"

"They move," she said.

"Do pencils move?" I asked.

"Yes! Pencils move. They move when you write with them, and sometimes they roll around all on their own."

Kate had discovered a way that pencils and bicycles are alike— they both move. That showed flexible thinking. On the surface, pencils and bicycles aren't at all alike, yet by stretching her logical imagination, Kate had discovered something the two objects had in common. My comments helped her along the way.

Once Kate was looking for an alikeness between a computer and a daisy. She was having trouble with this one. It seemed like a good time to engage her in a bit of negative thinking.

"Kate," I said, "instead of finding something a computer and a daisy both *can* do, let's find something a computer and a daisy *cannot* do. What's something a computer cannot do?"

"A computer can't breathe," she said.

"True. A computer doesn't breathe, but a daisy does. We need something that a computer doesn't do *and* a daisy doesn't do."

"A computer doesn't eat," she suggested.

"Yes, but daisies do," I said.

"A daisy doesn't eat popcorn," she said with a giggle.

"You're right. Daisies don't eat popcorn. Computers don't eat popcorn. We found it! A computer and a daisy are alike because neither of them eats popcorn."

A silly solution, but fun.

MR. YUM'S COOKIES

Mr. Yum is a cookie maker. Mr. Yum makes all kinds of cookies. He gives each variety of cookie a special name. These are all zoomies:

None of these are zoomies:

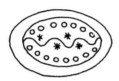

Think about zoomies. What do they have in common? How do they differ from non-zoomies?

Now look at these cookies. One of them is a zoomie. Which one?

How do you tell a zoomie from a non-zoomie? You must evaluate zoomie characteristics. You have to decide which attributes a zoomie must have and which attributes are not zoomie-like. Do zoomies have stripes? Some do, some don't. A stripe does not a zoomie make. Are zoomies round? Yes, all zoomies are round. But one of the non-zoomies is round too. Do zoomies have two swirls? Yes, all zoomies have two swirls. Do any of the non-zoomies have two swirls? No. Ah ha! Two swirls make a zoomie. It's only logical.

Now that you know what makes a zoomie, take a look at Mr. Yum's snippers:

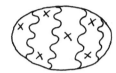

Look at these non-snippers:

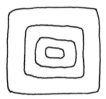

One of these is a snipper. Which one?

The first cookie, of course. It has X's *and* wavy stripes. That's what makes it a snipper.

Logic can get pretty strenuous in Mr. Yum's cookie kitchen. Your child must use logic to figure out the zoomie. You must use logic to make the problems.

Here's how to do it. First, think of a funny word: *shoodle*, for instance. Now decide what makes a shoodle a shoodle. Maybe all shoodles are star-shaped. In that case, here are three shoodles:

Here are three non-shoodles:

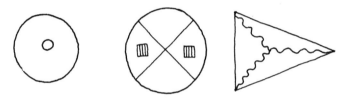

Here are two non-shoodles and one shoodle:

Your job is done. Now your child takes on the shoodle identification task.

Before you start making Mr. Yum's cookies on your own, you might enjoy some premade ones. At the end of this activity you'll find three sets of ready-to-puzzle-out cookies for your house. Just show your child the book, or copy the cookies onto another sheet of paper, and you're set. After finishing these samples, you're on your own.

As you play the game, you'll discover that some of Mr. Yum's cookies are easier to identify than others. It depends on the number of necessary and exclusive attributes in your drawing. Occasionally your child may identify a characteristic that works but which you didn't think of. This happened to me once while playing with Kate. I drew all the zoomies with green chips and none of the non-zoomies with green chips. I hadn't planned it that way. I hadn't even noticed what I'd done. To her credit, Kate did notice. This extra characteristic—zoomies have green chips—made finding the final zoomie an impossible task. My part of the game was a failure. I was embarrassed. That can happen. But Kate was kind and didn't tease me too much.

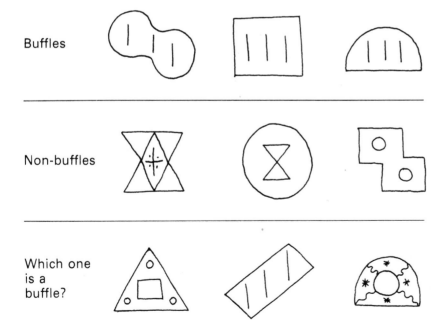

Buffles

Non-buffles

Which one
is a
buffle?

Fizzets

Non-fizzets

Which
one
is
a
fizzet?

Cluffs

Non-cluffs

Which
one
is a
cluff?

34

A pattern is an orderly, sequential, systematic, and logical method of organization. The number system is made up of endless patterns. Here's a lovely one:

$$1 \times 1 = 1$$
$$11 \times 11 = 121$$
$$111 \times 111 = 12{,}321$$
$$1{,}111 \times 1{,}111 = 1{,}234{,}321$$

Can you predict the answer to $11{,}111 \times 11{,}111$?

Mathematicians are fascinated by patterns, and discovering patterns is a major tool of mathematical problem-solving. Mathematicians aren't alone. Astronomers use patterns of orbiting planets to discover new information about our solar system. Medical researchers look for patterns in cell behavior to discover cures for diseases. Music and poetry move us emotionally in part through rhythmic patterns. Clearly, the ability to decode and decipher patterns is a fundamental aspect of intellectual life.

FIX IT is a game that makes searching out patterns fun for children. Why? Because FIX IT gives children the chance to catch adults making mistakes. That's why Millie liked the game so much. I drew a patterned sequence of shapes on a sheet of paper, and somewhere in the sequence I made a mistake.

Millie had two jobs. First she had to find my mistake. Then she had to draw the pattern correctly.

FIX IT

GRADES

kindergarten, first, and second

MATERIALS

paper
pencil

This game demanded a lot of Millie. She had to understand my pattern thoroughly; she had to identify my mistake; she had to make the correction. Sometimes she couldn't find the error. When this happened, I asked her to say out loud the shapes she saw. Saying the words *square, circle, circle, square, circle, circle, square, circle, circle, circle, square* helped her notice the extra circle.

The game demanded something from me too. I had to come up with the patterns. I always started with easy designs, moved to harder ones, and later, when she got quite adept, advanced to fiendishly tricky designs. Here's a collection of patterns (mistakes included) that you can copy if you don't want to make up your own:

Easy Patterns

Harder Patterns

Fiendishly Tricky Patterns

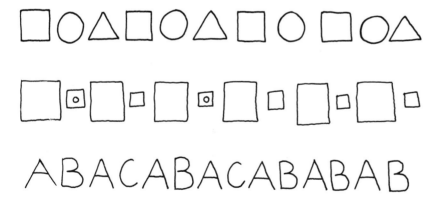

When Millie got to the point of doing fiendishly tricky patterns, I still gave her some of the easier patterns to do. There's no point in making every hill an Everest.

PATTERN GRIDS

GRADES

first, second, and third

MATERIALS

paper
pencil
crayons or colored pencils

*T*he patterns in the previous game, FIX IT, move in a single direction—left to right. In PATTERN GRIDS, they roam in many directions—left to right, top to bottom, diagonally. Designing the patterns can get a bit complicated, but it is also fun. To play, you must start with a grid.

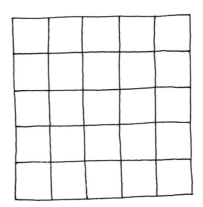

Then you fill each box of your grid, following a pattern. Fill in the first row, for instance, with a two-shape pattern: circle, triangle, circle, triangle, circle. Fill in the second row with a different pattern: flower, diamond, flower, diamond, flower. Return to circles and triangles for the third row. As you continue alternating patterns row by row, your grid will ultimately look like this:

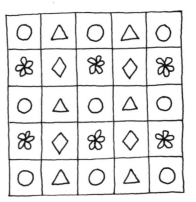

Now, for a bit of color, tint all the circles green, the triangles yellow, the flowers red, and the diamonds blue. Can you see patterns moving from left to right? Can you see patterns moving from top to bottom? Can you see patterns moving diagonally across the grid? One grid—lots of patterns.

Here's a second design, more sophisticated than the first:

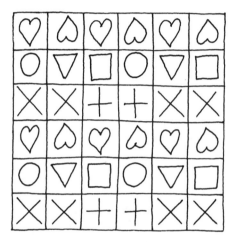

Instead of shapes, you can use letters. Here's a grid filled with the word *gum* repeated over and over, left to right, line to line:

G	U	M	G	U
M	G	U	M	G
U	M	G	U	M
G	U	M	G	U
M	G	U	M	G

Look carefully and you'll see an extraordinary number of patterns:

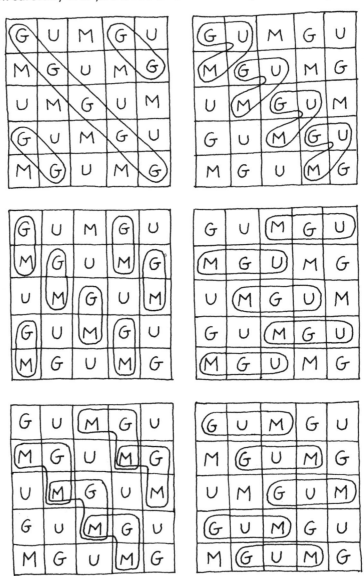

You can see the patterns more vividly if you color the grid.

You can change the size of the grid too. Here's a long, thin grid with a *mouse* inside, written left to right, top to bottom:

m	o	u
s	e	m
o	u	s
e	m	o
u	s	e
m	o	u
s	e	m

You can make grids with your name, your child's name, or your dog's name.

F	i	d	o	F	i	d	o	F	i
d	o	F	i	d	o	F	i	d	o
F	i	d	o	F	i	d	o	F	i
d	o	F	i	d	o	F	i	d	o

When you play this game, you can either work together on a single grid or make two grids, one for you and one for your child. With two grids, you invent one pattern, your child invents another. Then share the creations, studying the grids intently to see how many patterns you can pick out. Your designs may be more sophisticated than your child's, which is good. By using your work as a model, your child will develop his talents for discerning and creating patterns. In the meantime, you're sure to get some lovely pattern pictures to hang on your walls.

PART TWO
READ AND WRITE

chapter 3

Word Power

Lynn, the daughter of a friend, had just started first grade. I asked her what was the most special thing about being a first-grader. "I'll learn to read!" she said.

"That is special," I said. "Would you like to learn some words right now?"

"Okay," Lynn answered.

I pointed to the label on the juice carton. "Can you guess what these words say?" I asked.

"Orange juice?" she asked me back.

"Right. You just read two words: *orange* and *juice*. I'll write them on a paper for you, then you can read *orange juice* to your mom and dad."

Lynn was delighted with this plan. As soon as her mom walked into the room, Lynn ran to her shouting, "Look, I can read. See, this says *orange juice*, and I can read it."

Learning to read is, unfortunately, a bit more complicated than memorizing two words on a piece of paper. Still, Lynn had made an important first step. She'd experienced the powerful feeling of looking at letters on a page and deriving meaning from them. She had begun her lessons with a success. She was excited. In this chapter you'll find four games that will encourage such useful excitement in reading: A LABEL A DAY, I-CAN-READ-IT BOX, WORD LINKS, and LETTER-WRITING CAMPAIGN.

The chapter also includes three other games, which serve a different function. They help your child memorize the words he'll read most often in his life. A mere 400 words, as researchers have discovered, account for approximately 65 percent of all words found in books. Imagine! Once your child masters those crucial *in*s, *and*s, *of*s, not to mention *the*s, he'll be on his way. You can play any of these games in ten minutes or less, start to finish. Yet in that brief time, you'll give your child a definite boost in reading.

A LABEL A DAY

Play A LABEL A DAY with your child and after a few weeks the child's room will look like this:

G R A D E S

kindergarten and first

M A T E R I A L S

file cards or paper
pencil or pen
masking tape
optional: colored pencil

The room is covered, absolutely covered with labels. The bed is labeled *bed*. The chair is labeled *chair*. The toys, books, and doorknob are labeled. There are labels on the walls and on the floor.

How will this happen? Every day or so, you and your child will decide on a new label for the child's room. You'll write the word on a file card or piece of paper. Then you'll tape the label in place. Some days, if your child is interested, he can write the label. If he's too young to write independently, you can write the letters with light pencil strokes and the child can trace over your work with a darker line or with a colored pencil.

If your child likes this activity and you don't mind, let the labels overflow into other rooms: the kitchen, the bathroom, the living room.

How does this simple activity help children learn to read? It's exciting for young children to discover that room furnishings can become written words. Because each label is attached to a known object, the child can go around his room reading. It feels great to read *chair*, *bed*, and *table* with no help from Mom, Dad, or sarcastic older sisters. Some children will make interesting observations about words. They'll notice *desk* and *door* begin with the same sound and also with the same letter. What a coincidence! The same is true for *window* and *wall*, as well as for *floor* and *flower*. Older children build up their reservoir of memorized words by looking repeatedly at the labels. If you see a difficult word like *bureau* often enough in your bedroom, or *refrigerator* daily in your kitchen, it's easier to read these words when they show up in books at school.

Soon enough the labels will rip or fall down. By that time, however, those little cards will have done a big job helping your child learn to read.

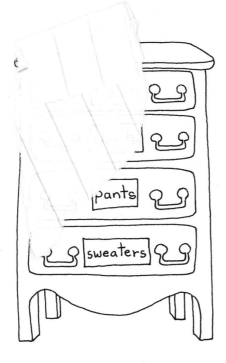

I-CAN-READ-IT BOX

GRADES

kindergarten and first

MATERIALS

file cards
file box
pencil or pen
crayons or colored pencils

Most first-graders are eager to read, but Joanna was especially so. Joanna's older brother could read fluently. He could read his favorite books whenever he felt like it. He didn't have to beg grown-ups for just one more story. What's more, Joanna's mom and dad were always bragging about him: Joey, the great reader. Joanna wanted the same success for herself. In her mind, entry into first grade meant automatic reading and an end to the inequality between herself and Joey. On day one of school, Joanna informed me, the school reading specialist, that she expected to read before the week was out.

A sizable demand, but in a small way not impossible to satisfy. The next day, Joanna poked her head into my workroom, and I had something special for her. I handed her a package wrapped in gift paper. Joanna tore off the paper and discovered a file box.

"What's this?" she asked.

"It's an I-CAN-READ-IT BOX, and it's just for you. All year long we'll fill it with words you can read. We're going to start today, right now. Pick any word you want, I'll write it down, and we'll put it in your I-CAN-READ-IT BOX."

"Good. I like it. But I don't know what word to use," Joanna said.

I made suggestions. "How about a favorite color: red, blue, purple. Or an animal: tiger, kangaroo, kitten. How about a favorite food: pizza, ice cream. Or a scary monster: witch, werewolf, vampire."

Joanna pondered the suggestions. Then she asked, "Can I do *butterfly*? I like butterflies."

"Sure, that's a fine choice," I said as I wrote the word *butterfly* on a file card. "Now can you read this word?" I asked.

"Butterfly."

"You did it, Joanna. You're beginning to read. You read *butterfly*. That's great. Come back tomorrow and we'll add a new word to your box. Soon you'll have a box full of words you can read."

Joanna was delighted and went smiling out of my workroom, chanting, "Butterfly, butterfly, butterfly."

The next day Joanna came prepared. She announced, "I want *puppy* today."

"That's a wonderful word," I said while writing. After the card was ready, I held it up and asked, "Can you read your new word?"

"It says *puppy*."

"That's it. Now, can you read yesterday's word?" I asked, holding up the card.

"It says *butterfly*."

"Right again. I'm going to mix up the cards. Let's see if, after they're mixed up, you can still read them both." I mixed, then held up *puppy*. Joanna read it. Next I held up *butterfly*, and she read that word too.

The following day she was ready for a new word. After that I slowed the pace. Instead of adding a word every day, we added words every other day, or every third day. I didn't want Joanna to get bored or overwhelmed by too many new words.

Sometimes Joanna asked to write the word herself. She was a little shaky when it came to forming letters so I wrote first in very light pencil strokes and she traced over the letters using a colored pencil. Other times she wrote the word all by herself with just a bit of spelling help from me. Sometimes Joanna was moved to draw pictures illustrating her words. By the end of the month Joanna had many words in her box. Most of these words she could read on sight. A few she couldn't remember at all. Occasionally she developed an aversion to a word. That happened with *shell*. Joanna decided *shell* wasn't worthy of her box. She wanted to throw it away. That was okay with me. I wanted the box to be full of exciting words. If that meant throwing out a card now and again, so be it.

Joanna spent a few moments of every day reading her word collection. Holding the gray file box steadily before her, she felt grown-up—sophisticated. She was justifiably proud of her increasing skill with words. One day she asked permission to take her box home.

"I want Joey to hear me read all these words," she declared. "He'll never believe it!"

WORD LINKS

GRADES

first and second

MATERIALS

paper
pencil

*T*ommy was in second grade and having a hard time learning to read. After a few tutoring sessions, I knew what we had to tackle. Because of his difficulties, reading was no fun for Tommy. Whenever he looked at words on a page, he cringed. His eyes glazed over. How could he make any headway when words made him feel so miserable? I tried some of my best games to excite Tommy about reading, but nothing worked. Then one day I drew eleven linked circles on a piece of paper. Like this:

I told Tommy to say the first word that came into his mind. Tommy looked at me a bit quizzically, then his eyes drifted to my hand, and he said *pencil*. I wrote the word in the first circle. Then I said: "Now I must write the first word that comes to my own mind when I think of *pencil*. I know, *hand*." I wrote this word in the second circle. "What word does *hand* bring to your mind, Tommy?"

Tommy answered, "*Foot*." I wrote *foot* in the third circle.

"Foot, foot, foot . . . that makes me think of *run*," I said, and I wrote the word. "What does *run* make you think of?"

"*Gym*," Tommy practically shouted.

I put *gym* in the fifth circle and then added my next contribution: *basketball*. Tommy responded with *net*. I followed with *tennis*. Tommy said *racket*. I retorted *noise*. Laughing aloud, Tommy came back with *thunder*.

Once I had filled all the circles with words, the page looked like this:

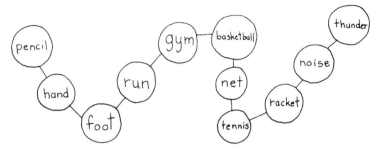

It had taken us just eleven words to travel from *pencil* to *thunder*. I started reading through the list pointing to each word as I read. Tommy was smiling and remembering the train of thought that led us on this route. By the time I read *basketball*, Tommy joined me in reading the words. We both agreed this game was a lot of fun. We were ready to play again, and I started drawing another set of circles—when the doorbell rang, signaling the end of Tommy's tutoring time. Tommy let out a groan of disappointment, but I promised we would play WORD LINKS first off next time we worked. He left the room, and I was astonished. He was actually looking forward to playing a reading game.

Why had this activity worked when others failed? First, it was fun to see how our thoughts moved from *pencil* to *thunder*—how odd. Second, because Tommy was as interested in my stream of consciousness as I was in his, our attention was riveted throughout the game. Third, Tommy could see that there were eleven and only eleven circles. Eleven circles—eleven words—such a reading assignment didn't seem too difficult. He wasn't overwhelmed or intimidated. What's more, each word led to the next in an interesting fashion, making the words easier to remember. They weren't "baby" words, either. They were power-packed words like *basketball* and *thunder*.

Mostly, the game worked because, luckily, Tommy liked it. Good teaching depends on many devices, and one of these devices is chance.

According to researchers, approximately 400 words account for about 65 percent of all written material. Clearly, if children recognize these words on sight, they'll have an easier time reading. What are these words? In the Appendix, you'll find a list of 477 common words. The list is broken down into three parts: Beginning Words, Intermediate Words, and Hotshot Words.

How can you help your child learn these words? You could force him to sit and study flash cards until he hates both you and reading. Or you could play games that make it fun to master words. That's the idea behind ROADBLOCK, which is a great game for children in the last half of first grade and throughout second and third grades.

On a blank sheet of paper, draw a road subdivided into fifteen sections, like this:

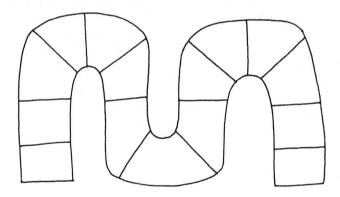

or this:

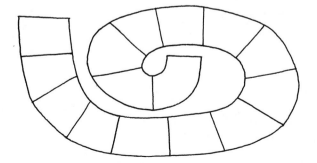

ROADBLOCK

GRADES
first, second, and third

MATERIALS
paper
pencil
a small game token

or this:

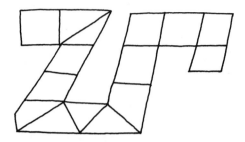

In each section of the road, write a word from the list in the Appendix. Fill some sections with Beginning Words: for instance, *can*, *he*, *if*, *like*, *girl*, *home*, *yellow*, *her*, and *out*. Fill other sections with Intermediate Words such as *leg*, *tree*, *store*, and *keep*. You can even fill a space or two with Hotshots like *across* and *beginning*. Read each word aloud for your child. Give him a moment to study the words. Then challenge him to travel down the road. To make this trip, he must read words. He starts in the first section of the road. If he can read that word, he moves on to the second section, and if he reads that word, it's on to the third section. He can mark his progress with any little object, a paper clip, for instance. Miniature cars are, of course, the best of all possible markers, though some children may prefer, say, a tiny horse. What happens when your child hits a word he can't read? Why, that's a ROADBLOCK.

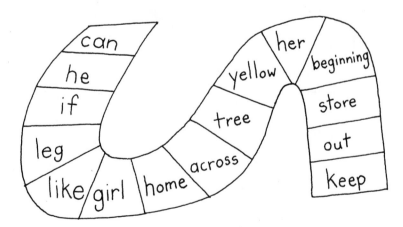

To make the blocked passage vivid, lower your finger—*boom*—across the board.

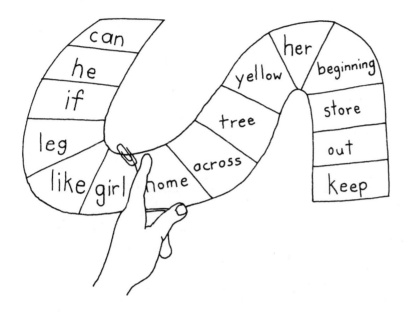

Say the word aloud. The child repeats it after you and studies the written word. Then it's back to the beginning to start the trip all over again. Your child has three chances to reach the end of the road. If he makes it, he wins the game. If he doesn't, you win.

After your child masters one road, make another road with new words. The more you play, the more words the child learns. Soon enough, Beginning Words will be too easy, Intermediate Words will be a snap, and even Hotshots will have cooled off.

PYRAMID

GRADES

first, second, and third

MATERIALS

paper
pencil
crayons

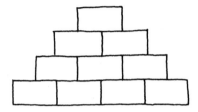
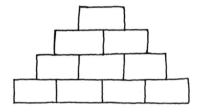

Variety—that's the key to helping children learn. The same old thing, day after day, will never do when it comes to the toughest tasks. How, for instance, to memorize the 477 words in the Appendix of this book? ROADBLOCK helps, certainly. But when you're tired of ROADBLOCK, give PYRAMID a chance.

You start by drawing two pyramids like these:

One pyramid is for you and one is for your child. Now turn to the List of Important Words. Pick a Beginning Word and write it on a piece of paper. Challenge your child to read the word before you count to ten. Count silently so you don't distract him. If he can read the word in ten seconds, he gets to color a block of his pyramid. If he can't, you read the word and color a block of your pyramid. Now choose a new word. You can pick another Beginning Word, but you might select an Intermediate or even a Hotshot. Keep picking words until either you or your child fully colors a pyramid and wins the game.

In general, try to confront your child with just one or two unknown words per game. If your child has trouble with the first two words you select, pick easier words for the remainder of the play. Your child needs to practice these words also. The more he does so, the faster and better a reader he'll become. Naturally, this means your child will almost always win the game. That's okay. After all, you're winning too when you help him become a stronger reader.

MADE TO ORDER

Sylvia was the youngest child in her second-grade class. If she'd been born one month later, she would have waited another year to begin school. This was the root of Sylvia's problem. She was a bit too young and unprepared during most of first grade and didn't learn what she should have learned. Still, the year ended and she went on to second grade. But she needed help. She needed to catch up.

She needed, above all, to memorize more words. Faced with a second-grade book, she resorted to sounding out word after word, and she read, therefore, in a painfully slow fashion. Sometimes sounding out was no use. Many of the most common words, *want*, *have*, *been*, for instance, don't follow the rules for spelling and sounding. Sylvia simply needed to memorize these and dozens of words like them. A vast job! So we played games. PYRAMID and ROADBLOCK were useful games, but MADE TO ORDER was her favorite. It only took a few minutes, but the few minutes once or twice a week produced terrific results. She memorized, she advanced, and after a few months of regular playing, she was pretty much at second-grade level, even if her reading was still not quite flawless.

I started the game by writing four words on a piece of paper.

away girl do house

Then I read the words to Sylvia, slowly, one at a time, pointing to each as I read. Sylvia read the words back to me, pointing as she went. This was pregame preparation. Now came the tricky part. I had to tell a little story using all four words in exactly the same order as on the page. I could use the different words as many times as I wanted, so long as the first mention of each word was in proper sequence. Every time I said a MADE TO ORDER word, I had to point to it on the paper.

A witch flew *away* from a little *girl* because the girl had her very own magic wand. The girl shouted after the witch, "*Do* not go or I will turn your *house* into a sand castle." But the witch didn't listen. So the girl took her wand and turned the house into sand. The witch cried and cried. She cried so much, her tears became an ocean. Suddenly, a huge ocean wave swept away the sand castle. The witch stamped her foot hard—so hard that she sank in the sand and disappeared forever.

This was not, perhaps, the cleverest story ever told. Nevertheless, it held Sylvia's attention.

Next, Sylvia had to come up with a story, a different one from mine, although she could use my plot for inspiration. Sylvia had to include *away*, *girl*, *do*, and *house* in her story—in proper order. What's more, she had to point to each word on the paper as she used it in her tale. This was a hard job, but Sylvia enjoyed it.

How did I pick MADE TO ORDER words? Mostly I used the List of Important Words in the Appendix. When we first began playing, I used Beginning Words. Slowly I added Intermediate Words, and eventually Hotshots. Along with these basic words, I occasionally threw in an exotic extra like *Halloween* or *baboon*. Once Sylvia was really accomplished at the game, we'd play with five or six words instead of just four. At this point I let Sylvia pick a few of the game words. She could choose any word she wanted, from the list or from her own imagination, from *allosaurus* (a kind of dinosaur) to *zombie* (a living dead person).

allosaurus
out
zombie
must

Now that's a wild MADE TO ORDER combination. Would you care to give it a try?

It's time for you to go out for the evening. Your child's favorite baby-sitter is already in the house. Before you leave, take a few minutes to write a letter:

> Hello, Sweetie,
> I bet you had a good time tonight with Sherry. Did you play checkers? Did you watch TV? Tomorrow morning you can tell us all about it. See you then.
> Love and kisses,
> Mom and Dad

Stick this note on your child's pillow all ready for her to read before she goes to sleep.

It's time for school. You're getting a sandwich and chips ready for your daughter's lunch box. Stop and take a few minutes to write a letter:

> Hi there!
> Here's your favorite lunch: peanut butter and honey. Did you share your rock collection at morning meeting? I bet everyone liked that red one. It's special—just like you.
> See you tonight after after-school.
> I love you,
> Dad

Stick this note into the lunch box, ready for your child to read at school.

GRADES

first, second, and third

MATERIALS

paper
pencil

You're leaving for work, but before you walk out the door, write a letter:

Hi!

How was school today? I hope you had fun. I hope you learned a lot. Did Ms. Gatto read more in *Charlotte's Web*? When I get home, you can tell me what Wilbur did today.

There's a snack in the refrigerator. Don't eat cookies before dinner!

See you soon.

Mom

Stick the note on the refrigerator door, all set for your child's return from school and that visit to the refrigerator.

Why engage in this letter writing? Because your child may really enjoy this special communication with you; because these notes make reading an everyday part of your child's life; because letters from you may increase your child's interest in reading; because, although these notes will only take you a few minutes to write, they will accomplish so much.

How often should you write letters? Once a week, once a day, whenever you go out for the evening—whatever works best for you. Try to keep the language simple, but don't worry about the vocabulary too much. Kids can usually catch the drift of a note even if they can't read every word on the page. What's more, the child's teacher or baby-sitter can always help if the note is too difficult to understand.

chapter 4

Sounds Abound

Flox rumpish slaption. Can you say this "sentence"? Probably you can and with perfect pronunciation. In all probability, you've never seen *flox*, *rumpish*, or *slaption* before, given that they don't exist, so how do you know their sounds? You know rules that govern pronunciation. You know how to use letter sounds to read words. You can blend these sounds into words. You possess a great wealth of phonetic skills. Of course, adults rarely use these skills, having automatic recall of virtually all the words they read. Not so with your child. A child must sound out the syllables.

Learning all the rules that govern written English—and all the exceptions to the rules—is an enormous task. Look at this list: *top*, *noon*, *foot*, *boy*, *out*, *no*, *some*. Each word has an *o*, and each *o* has a different sound. *Boy* and *oil* have an identical vowel sound, but the sound is made with different combinations of letters. Children learning Turkish need only master twenty-seven symbols representing twenty-seven sounds. In English we have 379 letters and combinations of letters to make a minimum of forty sounds. What a mess!

Even when a child knows the letter sounds in isolation, he may still have problems. He may find it difficult to blend separate sounds into a single word. Knowing the three sounds *ccc . . . aaa . . . ppp . . .* is not the same as being able to say *cap*. Children need practice.

The games in this chapter are the practice. A game here, a game there makes sounding out phun and eezee.

MYSTERY WORDS

Molly looked at a new word: *mat*. She began to attack the word sound by sound. *"Mmmmm . . . aaaaa . . . ttttt . . . What's that?"*

Many beginning readers would sympathize with Molly. It's hard to blend isolated and S-T-R-E-T-C-H-E-D O-U-T sounds into familiar words. MYSTERY WORDS can help.

To begin the game, I assigned Molly the role of detective and myself the role of MYSTERY WORDS maker.

"Are you ready, Word Detective, to tackle your first mystery word?" I said, trying to set up the proper suspense-filled mood. "All right, here we go." I pronounced the three stretched-out sounds: *"Sssss . . . iiiii . . . ppppp . . ."* and I asked, "Can you blend these sounds into a word? Can you solve the mystery? Can you tell me the mystery word?"

Molly repeated the sounds. She shook her head, confused. She asked to hear the sounds again. I repeated them, but with less of a stretch: *"Ss . . . ii . . . pp . . ."*

Molly giggled and blurted out, "Sip, sip, sip. I solved it! I solved the mystery word!"

Yes, she had, and we were both very pleased. Molly, in fact, was so pleased that she wanted another round of MYSTERY WORDS right away. Then another and another. After five words and three minutes we called it quits, since there's no point in overdoing a good thing. Remember, there's always ttt-ooo-mmm-ooo-rrr-ooo-www.

I'm thinking of something you wear on your head. It rhymes with *sat*. What can it be?

I'm thinking of the place where you find cows and chickens. It rhymes with *arm*. What can it be?

I'm thinking of something you find in a living room. It rhymes with *air*. What can it be?

This is RIDDLE RHYMES. Half a dozen rounds of this game take less than half a dozen minutes to play. Here's what happens in those few minutes. Your child looks for something in the living room that rhymes with *air*. He begins listing furnishings. He starts with *couch*. Does *couch* rhyme with *air*? *Couch—air—couch—air*. Rhymeless. How about *table*? Does it rhyme with *air*? No. Well, how about *chair*? *Chair—air—chair—air*. That's a rhyme. Thinking like this helps any child rhyme in time.

Why bother with learning to rhyme? Children who detect the relationship between *tap*, *nap*, and *cap* enjoy a distinct advantage in reading. Often they can decipher words they've never seen before, like *sap* or *gap*, sometimes without a moment's thought. It's because they notice the connection between the rhyming sound and the letters *ap*. And there's a second, more general reason too. Rhyming builds a sensitivity to sounds. It takes a sharp ear to tell that *tap* and *lap* rhyme and *tap* and *lab* do not. These little distinctions are everything in reading.

HIDE-AND-SEEK SOUNDS

GRADES

kindergarten and first

MATERIALS

four index cards
or four pieces of paper
pencil

Hide-and-seek is usually played by hiding in a closet, but there's no reason why the game shouldn't take on a slightly phonetic quality. When I played with Lauren, I began by taking four index cards and writing a single letter—*m*, *d*, *f*, *g*—on each card. The letters were always consonants. Vowels don't work in this game.

Then I told Lauren to close her eyes while I hid the cards around the room. Behind a couch pillow, I hid the *g* card—leaving a white corner out in plain view. I hid *d* under the telephone—with a tiny tip sticking out. I hid *f* on top of the television and *m* behind a lamp.

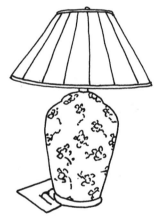

I told Lauren to open her eyes and said, "Somewhere hidden in this room is the letter that makes the sound *mmmmmmm*. Look, look, and look until you find it. If you have trouble, I'll give you hints."

"*Mmmmm,*" said Lauren. "I know that letter. That's *m.* Don't worry, I can find it." Lauren began hunting. She skipped to the bookshelf and started taking out a book.

"No, Lauren," I said, "all the cards are in sight. You don't have to empty shelves or open drawers."

"Okay," she said, and began poking around the couch. "I see something," she shrieked. She grabbed the card behind the pillow. "It's not *m.* It's *g.*"

"Oh, well," I said sympathetically. "Put it back where you found it. You'll be looking for the *gggg* sound soon enough. How about a hint to help you find *mmmm?*"

"Okay," she said.

"You're a bit warm now, but you were warmer over by the bookshelf." Lauren headed back to the books. "You're getting warmer—and warmer—and warmer. You're almost hot. Oh no, turning toward the door made you colder—and colder."

I kept cooling Lauren off and warming her up until she looked behind the lamp and found the card with *m.* "You found *mmmm.* Hooray! Now can you find the letter that makes *ffff?*"

Lauren returned to the hunt. In less than ten minutes she'd found all four cards. Lauren asked to play another round, but we needed to go on to other things. I promised her that in a day or so we'd play again, using different letters.

In short order, Lauren could match each consonant with its proper sound, from the easy ones like *t* to letter sounds that even adults find difficult, like *q* (*kw*) and *x* (*ks*). She even knew that *c* has two sounds, as does *g.* Lauren would have despised sitting quietly in a chair memorizing letter sounds—but she was delighted to snoop around my living room learning each and every one.

FIRST SOUND, LAST SOUND

GRADES

first and second

MATERIALS

paper
pencil
small snack (raisins or peanuts)

Yvonne came to her tutoring sessions directly from school. She was usually hungry, so I had peanuts, her favorite snack, ready for her. Initially, we spent this time chatting about the latest news at school. After a few weeks, however, I began experimenting with games to turn snack time into learning time. Our most successful snack game was FIRST SOUND, LAST SOUND. When we played this game, Yvonne never complained about working while snacking.

I had to prepare a FIRST SOUND, LAST SOUND game board. This was a piece of paper with a line drawn down the middle and the heading FIRST on one side and LAST on the other.

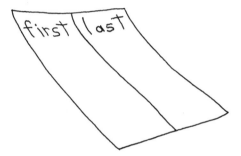

Board complete, we were ready to play. To start things off, I asked Yvonne where she heard the sound *ffff* in the word *fudge.* Was it the first sound or the last sound? Instead of answering me in words, Yvonne took a peanut and placed it on the FIRST side of the game board.

"Way to go, Yvonne," I said. "*Ffff* is the first sound in *fudge*. You get to eat that peanut anytime you want."

Yvonne grabbed the peanut and started to chew. "That was easy, easy, easy," she said between bites.

"Are you ready for your next word?" I asked.

Yvonne was ready, and so I asked where she heard the *ssss* sound in *snake*. She won another peanut. I asked about the *nnnn* sound in *dragon*, the *llll* sound in *hole* (it's the sound, not the spelling that counts), and the *gggg* sound in *goofy*. Unfortunately, Yvonne goofed on *goofy*. I took a peanut off the board and returned it to the bowl. I gave her a chance to reclaim the peanut, however, by finding the *wwww* sound in *wood*. We played for about ten minutes—or fifteen peanuts—and then went on to other work.

Eventually FIRST SOUND, LAST SOUND ceased to challenge Yvonne. She won all the peanuts easily. So I made the game harder. The new game board had three divisions: FIRST, MIDDLE, and LAST.

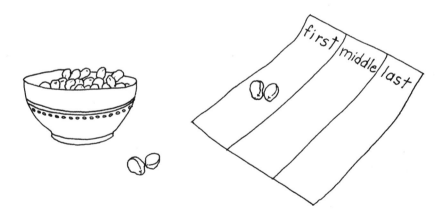

To get her peanut, Yvonne had to answer questions about the first sound, the last sound, and the middle sound. Where's the *tttt* sound in *tunnel*? Where's the *tttt* sound in *ghost*? Where's the *pppp* sound in *computer*? Middle sounds are tricky and the game was harder, but Yvonne was ready, so it was more fun too.

Peanuts aren't absolutely necessary, and you don't even need a game board. You can simply ask your child FIRST SOUND, LAST SOUND questions and give points for success. When your child racks up ten or perhaps fifteen points, the game ends. A game board does make the game more official, though, and peanuts make it yummier.

Here's a list of FIRST SOUND, LAST SOUND words, followed by FIRST SOUND, MIDDLE SOUND, LAST SOUND words, to get you going:

First Sound, Last Sound

p sound in *pudding*	*s* sound in *mouse*
n sound in *nose*	*l* sound in *candle*
f sound in *safe*	*m* sound in *monster*
t sound in *pocket*	*v* sound in *stove*
ch sound in *child*	*v* sound in *violet*
w sound in *waffle*	*k* sound in *kangaroo*

First Sound, Middle Sound, Last Sound

b sound in *notebook*	*m* sound in *morning*
v sound in *cover*	*n* sound in *noodles*
ee sound in *green*	*b* sound in *table*
p sound in *sharp*	*n* sound in *lemon*
t sound in *kitten*	*m* sound in *lemon*

g sound in *giggle*
(a two-peanut word)

Keisha, a bright first-grader, was falling behind her class. It was March and the class had done a lot of work sounding out words, but Keisha still found this job unpleasantly difficult. One activity, however, put a smile on her face—SWITCHEROO. Here's how we played. I wrote a starter word on a piece of paper:

SWITCHEROO

GRADES

first, second, and third

MATERIALS

paper
pencil with an eraser

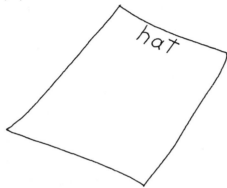

Then I challenged Keisha to read the word. That was easy; she could read *hat* automatically.

"Okay, Keisha, you've done the first part just fine. But in order to get a point in this game, you must read the SWITCHEROO word too. Here it is."

With that, I erased the *a* in *hat* and replaced it with a *u*. Now there was a new word, *hut*.

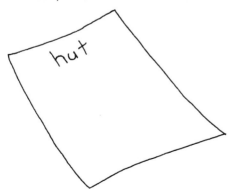

That's how SWITCHEROO works. You start with words like *cap*, *sit*, *bet*, and *lap*. These words have three letters with a vowel in the middle, and the vowel is always short (*a* as in *apple*, *e* as in *egg*, *i* as in *itch*, *o* as in *ox*, *u* as in *up*). Then you switch the vowels around and you end up with words like *cup*, *sat*, *but*, and *lip*. When your child reads both the first word and the SWITCHEROO word, you award a point. Otherwise the point goes to you. The first person with five points wins the game.

Keisha looked worried when I wrote *hut*. She didn't recognize the word, and she knew she would have to sound it out. Sounding out was exactly what dismayed her.

"Hhhh . . . that's the first sound," she proclaimed with confidence. "H-uh . . . huh . . . t—*hut*. That's the word, it's *hut*."

"Hooray, you got your first point! If you'd made a mistake, I'd have a point."

"I'm gonna get all the switcheroos today," Keisha said.

Her prediction almost came true. She missed one switch, beating me five to one. She was proud of winning. She was also proud of doing such a fine job sounding out words. Such hard work would have been boring and frustrating had it involved filling in blanks in a workbook. But sounding out words wasn't boring at all—it was even worth a bit of frustration—when it meant winning a game.

Here are three rings with letters in each ring:

GRADES

first, second, and third

MATERIALS

paper
pencil

Can you spell words using the letters in the rings? You must follow a few rules. The words should have three letters, and the first letters should come from the first ring, the second letter from the second ring, the third letter from the third. Proper names, like Pat or Sam, are permitted, but nonsense words are not.

Here's a word:

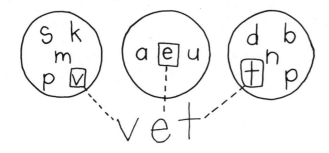

Here's another:

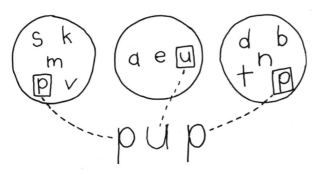

Words are worth points in THREE-RING WORD GAME. You can play cooperatively or competitively. In a cooperative game, you and your child work together to find words, thereby racking up as many points as you can. In a competitive game, you and your child work separately, writing words on your own sheets of paper. Each word gets one point. And any time the child lists a word that you, the grown-up, fail to put on your own list, the child gets an extra point.

English spelling, being somewhat unreliable, may create problems for your child in THREE-RING WORD GAME (as well as in life). Your child might put together three letters that "sound out" perfectly but are misspelled nevertheless: *sed* instead of *said*, *kup* instead of *cup*. When this happens, congratulate your child on hearing the sounds, then dolefully inform him that correct sounds do not always proper spellings make. In this game, sad to say, only correct spellings win points.

There's a useful way to deal with the most common spelling problems, however. To make the endings that sound like *k, f, s,* and *l*, we generally use two letters: *ck, ff, ss,* and *ll*. Once a child is familiar with the game, I put these two-letter sets in the third ring. That way, players can make words like *dock, puff, mess,* and *hill*, which have three sounds but four letters.

Here are some rings to get you and your child started:

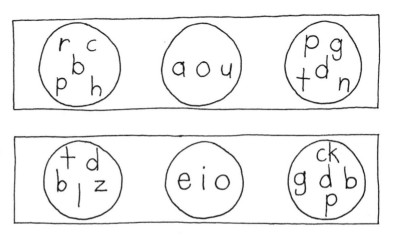

For accomplished ring leaders, you can add more vowels to the middle circle.

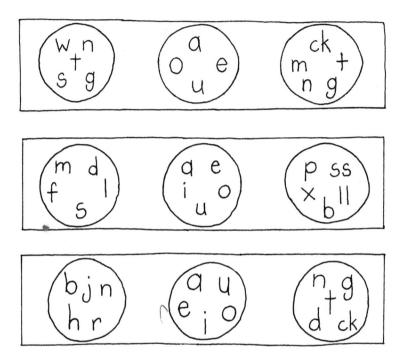

If you and your child like this game, play it in restaurants, on train trips, in laundromats, or any other place when you have ten minutes and a couple of sheets of paper. It's a fine way to help your child run rings 'round phonics.

FLIP A DIP WITH A DRIP AND SLIP

GRADES

second and third

MATERIALS

paper
pencil

Some children have a great deal of trouble sounding out words letter by letter. These youngsters find that breaking words into single-letter sounds is more confusing than helpful. This was the case with Roger, a very unhappy boy. Roger was in second grade. He had started first grade with great expectations. He'd worked hard all year. He hadn't made much progress in reading, however. Now he was in second grade, and his enthusiasm was lagging. He dreaded failing yet again.

How could I help Roger? I had only three choices. First, I could force him to sound out words even though he found it difficult and frustrating. Second, I could abandon phonics altogether as a way of teaching him to read. Or third, I could use a slightly different phonetic approach, one that showed Roger how to sound out words without going letter by letter. I chose the third possibility.

I showed Roger a set of rhyming words, all with the same sounds and the same letters: *lip, dip, drip, flip*. I read the list out loud, pointing to the *ip, ip, ip*. I hoped Roger would see a connection between the letters and the repeated rhyming sounds. Then I wrote the nonsense word *glip*. Could Roger read it? If he could, it would show he was beginning to make use of letter sounds when reading words. He wouldn't be doing this letter by letter: *g-l-i-p*. Instead, he would have identified a family of *ip* words and used this family to successfully sound out a word he'd never read before.

I held my breath. Roger read. He did it! He was reading nonsense without a wisp of trouble. Then I wrote *flipper* and *slipper*. Roger was delighted to discover that now he could read these hard words automatically. After a few list-of-rhyming-words lessons, the novelty began to wear off. How could I keep Roger learning and having fun simultaneously? Only a game would do. That's the origin of FLIP A DIP WITH A DRIP AND SLIP.

The first time we played, I wrote the following rhyming list:

"Roger," I said, "I'm going to make up a story using all these rhyming words. It may take me a second, so be patient."

Roger waited as I studied the list. In a minute I recited this silly ditty: "A hamburger *bun* went to sit in the *sun*. It was *fun* until he saw a *gun* and that made him *run*."

"Hey, that's neat," said Roger admiringly.

"Thanks," I said. "That's what's fun about this game, your stories can be really nutty. I bet you can do one that's just as crazy as mine—maybe even crazier. Want to try?"

"I don't know," he said.

"Would you like a new set of words?" I asked, feeling he'd respond more favorably if he wasn't in direct competition with me. I didn't wait for an answer. I just began writing: *cap, trap, map, slap*. Roger looked at the words and agreed to make up a story. He came up with this: "A *cap* with a *map* set a *trap* so he could *slap* a bad guy."

"That's super, Roger. You're really good at this game. How about selecting some rhyming words for me? No more than five words, though. I doubt I can handle more than five."

Roger smiled and rattled off *hum, gum, some, drum.* I wrote the words on a piece of paper to help him see the visual pattern that went along with the rhymes. True, *some* didn't fit the pattern, but that's life in the English language.

Then I made up a story: "A *drum* can *hum* with *some gum* in his toes."

"That stinks," said Roger.

"You're right, but it's the best I could do. Do you want to take a turn now?"

Roger did, and I wrote a new list: *snow, blow, row, know.* A minute later he had a story. "The *snow* can *blow.* I *know* you can *row* away."

Excellent—and I told Roger as much.

We'd finished this day's work with FLIP A DIP WITH A DRIP AND SLIP. Over the next several weeks we played the game for five minutes or so as Roger ate his snack. The silliness of the game appealed to Roger, and so he was happy to play again and again. It takes a long time for a good game to wear out. And since it sometimes takes a long time for a child to master an especially difficult topic, the attractiveness of this game was a lucky thing.

*C*ynthia, a third-grader, was reading well, though not perfectly. She had a good reading vocabulary, but when she came to a word that she didn't already know, she stumbled. She rarely tried to sound out the newcomer. Instead, she shrugged her shoulders and gave me a look that said, "You figure it out. It's too much for me." As long as she stayed with simple books that introduced only a few new words at a time, her reading was smooth enough. I knew, however, that in fourth grade she would be in for a shock. Because authors assume that older students can sound out new words, books written at a fourth-grade level introduce words at a fast and furious pace. Cynthia was not going to be able to sound out words well enough to meet the challenge.

Cynthia's talent for memorizing words made the task harder, not easier. The trick was to find words she couldn't possibly already know—nonsense words, for example. That way, she'd have to use phonetic clues to read the word. From the point of view of sounding out the letters, a made-up word like *smootish* is just as good as *smoothly*, and in Cynthia's case, *smootish*, being unknown, was better. So we embarked on a *smootish* word game, which we called NONSENSE STARS.

Here's how it worked. I drew two stars, one for Cynthia and one for me.

GRADES

second and third

MATERIALS

paper
pencils
optional: colored pencils

Cynthia's star   Peggy's star

Then I wrote a nonsense word for Cynthia to read. She had two chances to sound out the word. If she succeeded, she could color a section of her star, like this:

or this:

or this:

If she couldn't figure out the word, I colored part of my star. The first person to color a whole star won the game.

Cynthia's first nonsense word was *grop*. She read this with no trouble.

"Very impressive," I said. "How did you know how to read it?"

"Easy," she said. "It looks like *drop*, only there's a different beginning."

"I'd better be trickier if I want to win this game," I said. "Try this one." I wrote another nonsense word:

spinfepper

Unfortunately, *spinfepper* was too difficult. Cynthia was completely thrown by all the letters.

"Will you let me help you with this tough word?" I asked. Cynthia didn't object. "Here's what I'll do," I said. "I'll write the word again. Only this time I'll write it in little bits, syllable by syllable. I think that's fair, don't you?"

Cynthia nodded enthusiastically as I started writing.

spin   fep   per

I finished and Cynthia began. She read slowly, one syllable at a time, until she successfully deciphered the whole thing. Then she proudly colored a new part of her star.

Cynthia probably thought she'd had the better of me by getting me to provide extra help and letting her color in part of the star. But I'd actually helped her for my own reasons. Here was an opportunity to give her a lesson on breaking long words into small parts or syllables, which is a basic aspect of sounding out words. Cynthia needed this lesson, and playing with NONSENSE STARS was an easy way to get it. She wasn't bored, because the lesson was instantly practical: learning to syllabize words would help her win the game. And when she did win, she felt good about the game and about herself. Sounding out a word like *spinfepper* was not, after all, an easy thing to do. Newly confident, Cynthia continued sounding out nonsense words until she finished coloring her star. I did get one section of my star colored when Cynthia couldn't tackle *scrumpittle*, even after I broke it into syllables. Still, my partly colored star couldn't compare to Cynthia's fully colored beauty.

Sometimes, given the peculiarity of English spelling, there's more than one way to pronounce a word. I always gave Cynthia credit for any reading that sounded reasonable. Perfection wasn't the point of the game. The point was to give her practice in the principles of sounding out unknown words—breaking the word down into its parts, getting the sound of each part, blending the sounds together. And if she giggled in the process, so much the better.

Here's a list of nonsense words—starting with easy ones, then hard ones, and, finally, killers—to get your stars twinkling:

Easy	Hard	Killers
mem	pemment	remishpop
nep	bepbock	stipotter
closs	spoint	limpendish
semp	nouff	scriffellottom
dafe	lewper	toolmaph
lome	stoimt	cifferlopite
maish	poddemt	nuitleemptupe
floop	scolleck	umperstoremple

RUNAWAY LETTERS

C-n yo- rea- th-s? So-e l-tter-ha-e r-n -way. C-n you pu- th-m b-ck? If you can read these sentences and fill in the dashes with the correct letters, consider yourself a RUNAWAY LETTERS champ.

Would your child like to track down RUNAWAY LETTERS? There's one way to find out. Get a piece of paper and start writing. Begin with short sentences composed of simple words, and replace letters with dashes in just a few places: *I -ike your f-og.* After a child figures out the words, he uses his knowledge of letter sounds to replace the runaways. Gradually, you can make the sentences longer, leave out letters in more words, and occasionally leave out more than one letter in a word. A trained tracker can handle even this: *A b-g hung-y ti-er h-nted for l-ttle an-ma-s in the j-ng-e.*

This is another game in which the irregularity of English spelling can cause problems. What letter should you fill in here? *Br-ther.* You know the word and so you know the missing letter is *o.* However, if your child replaces the dash with a *u* on the grounds that the missing sound is the same as the *u* in *up,* he'd be right about sounds, even though he'd be wrong about spelling. When this happens—and it's bound to happen—congratulate your child on his fine ear for letter sounds and then bemoan the fate of English-language readers and writers who must suffer with such a mischievous language.

Your child may want to test your letter-tracking ability. He'll want to write words with dashes for you to decipher. Unfortunately, taking the writer's role in this game is harder than it looks, and your child might get frustrated after giving it a try. Here's something you can do to make it easier. Give your child a book, a magazine, a cereal box, or anything with words. Tell him to copy a sentence. Then let him blacken letters so that they're unreadable. The child hands you the paper and you must catch the runaways.

This is a ten-minute game, although many children will happily play longer. G- ahead, t-y a run-way t-da-.

chapter 5

Reading and Meaning

Chip or Mary—who was the better reader? I handed Mary a biography of Thomas Edison and listened while she read. She said every word quickly, effortlessly. I asked her to tell me about the story, however, and she just shrugged her shoulders. She'd read the words, but they had no meaning.

Another time, I gave Chip the same book. Chip struggled with many words, though eventually he could figure them out. When I asked him about the story, though, he recounted the tale flawlessly. The words were hard, but the book was meaningful. Who was the better reader? Chip. Chip comprehended the story, he didn't simply recite the words.

It's not enough to teach children to sound out words or help them recognize lots of words by sight. We must also help children understand what they read. If your child has a strong vocabulary, if he knows the meanings of words, he'll read better because of it. If your child understands that stories are somewhat predictable, that causal relations link events in the plot, that characters will have reasons for acting as they do, he'll be even better at reading. If your child reads with emotion, if he captures the correct tone of a story, he'll be better yet again. How can you make sure your child has these skills? The games in this chapter are a start.

SILLY WORDS, WHAT'S THE OPPOSITE? and WORD OF THE DAY help build your child's vocabulary. SAY IT WITH FEELING helps your child read with expression. CIRCLE STORY helps your child analyze plots and characters. READING ALOUD helps with everything.

SILLY WORDS

What does a good reader do when he stumbles on an unknown word? He uses a logical procedure.

First, the good reader uses letter sounds to figure out what's written. Sometimes that's enough, and the word stands revealed. Other times a second step is required. The sounds may give only a near approximation of the actual word. Think of *some*. If you sound it out correctly, it rhymes with *home*. The good reader doesn't worry, though. The good reader pays attention to the context in which the unknown word appears. Context together with the less-than-correct pronunciation may explain the word.

What happens, though, if the word isn't familiar—if the word, and not just the spelling, is unknown to the child? The youngster may sound out the new word correctly but not know the meaning. The good reader stays calm. The good reader understands that the word must make sense in the sentence, and tries to derive the meaning from the context.

See for yourself with this sentence: *The cat flooped the dish of milk, but she still wanted more.*

Did you figure out *flooped*? You probably pronounced it easily, but what meaning did you attribute to it? Perhaps you decided *flooped* means lapped, or slurped, or finished. Whatever your choice, you picked something that helped make sense of the cat's relation to the milk. That's what a good reader does. The next time you see *flooped*, the context may let you narrow down its meaning. Soon enough you'll have a good definition for *flooped*. That's how a child's vocabulary grows while reading.

What about the poor reader? The poor reader may use letter sounds to figure out words, but he's more likely to have problems getting the sounds exactly right. The poor reader must therefore rely on context to figure out difficult words. If the poor reader lacks this ability too, there's not much alternative but to take a wild guess. *Kitchen* becomes *kangaroo*; *mermaid* becomes *meatball*; the story becomes confusing.

How can you help your child figure out unknown words from the context of a story, the way good readers do? Try SILLY WORDS.

To begin the game, you start to tell a story. You can invent your own story, retell a fairy tale, or steal plots from the movies.

Once upon a time a little girl lived in the forest with her voomer.

Now ask your child to translate *voomer*. Can he do it? Accept any word that makes sense. You may have intended *voomer* to mean mother, but if your child substitutes father or grandmother or cat, well, go with it. Then continue the story:

The girl's mother made her a choil cape with a choil hood.

Can your child translate *choil*?

The mother made some treats for Grandmother. The little girl had to travel through the puckle and take the treats to Grandmother.

What can *puckle* mean? Can your child figure it out?

Keep up the story and keep up the SILLY WORDS until your tale is done.

If you and your child like SILLY WORDS, here are two variations you might also enjoy. Try playing the game when you are reading aloud from a storybook. Every now and again, instead of reading the word on the page, substitute a *fubble*, a *gwish*, or a *plud*. Then give your child a chance to translate the silly word into English.

Here's a second variation. Occasionally, while eating dinner, while doing chores, or on a lazy Sunday afternoon, throw a nonsense word into the conversation:

"Please trock the potatoes."
"Did you hubble your room?"
"Would you like to splach checkers?"

The first time you talk so crazily your child may be surprised and confused. Once your child gets used to the oddness, however, he may turn the tables on you and start jabbering nonsense. Don't be surprised. Don't be confused. Just squibbish with your son or your difmer for a few spootches.

Reading and Meaning

WHAT'S THE OPPOSITE?

*T*raveling on a train from New York City to Princeton, New Jersey, I overheard a father and daughter pass the time by playing a terrific game.

The father began by asking, "What's the opposite of soft?"

"Hard," answered the daughter. Then she asked a question. "What's the opposite of long?"

"Short," answered the father. "What's the opposite of early?"

"Late," the daughter answered. "What's the opposite of car?"

"I can't really think of something that's the opposite of a car. I can think of things that are different from cars, but that's not the same as opposite. Do you want to give me another?"

"Okay. What's the opposite of far?"

"That's a good one," said her father. "Let's see, the opposite of far is near. What's the opposite of merry?"

What a great game. It was simple. It was fun. It was developing the daughter's interest and delight in language. It was helping her understand some subtleties of vocabulary. It was giving her a feeling of control and ownership over words. Children who have good vocabularies and a strong interest in language have a big edge when it comes to understanding stories and books.

So I'm passing this game along to you. I hope you have as much fun with it as that father and daughter journeying through New Jersey. Just say, "What's the opposite of," and pick a word that might have an opposite.

If you like WHAT'S THE OPPOSITE? you'll probably enjoy its opposite too. Instead of searching for opposites, or antonyms, ask your child for likes, or synonyms. What's the same as silly? What's the same as full? What's the same as scared? What's the same as delightful? A few rounds like this, a little chatting, a glance out the window, and it's time to get off the train.

WORD OF THE DAY

When your child first learned to talk, you were besieged by a young voice asking over and over again, "What does that mean? What does that mean?" Your child needed more and more words in order to make sense of the world.

By first and second grade, most children know the words they hear in daily conversation. They're also familiar with the restricted vocabulary used in their schoolbooks. "What does that mean?" usually tapers off to a minimum.

By third and fourth grade, however, vocabulary reappears as an important issue. Children encounter unfamiliar words all the time in stories and books, which makes for problems.

You can't understand a story, after all, unless you know what the words mean. A child who enters the upper elementary grades with a big vocabulary clearly has an advantage.

Hence WORD OF THE DAY. Imagine yourself at dinner. The main course is over, dessert is on the way—now is a good time to play. Announce that you have a special word to share, your WORD OF THE DAY. Then pick a word—*radiant* is a good first choice. Your child may ask what it means, but don't tell him. Instead, use *radiant* in a sentence and dare your child to figure out the meaning. If he comes up with the correct definition, congratulate him on divining the meaning. If he doesn't, try a new sentence and see if that helps. If after three sentences he's still baffled, define the word for him. You've just introduced your child to a new word. You've also made thinking about vocabulary a family event, which is a good idea, so long as WORD OF THE DAY doesn't become a feared examination before dessert, which would defeat the idea.

On another evening, introduce a second WORD OF THE DAY. How do you decide on the word? There's only one prerequisite. The word must be unknown to your child. *Prerequisite*, for instance, is a likely candidate. If you have trouble coming up with a word, the dictionary is where to look. You can even make thumbing through the dictionary part of the game, which has the benefit of introducing children to the morsels contained in that amazing book. If a dictionary is unavailable, skim through books, magazines, or newspapers. You're sure to find just the right WORD OF THE DAY.

SAY IT WITH FEELING

Charlene read aloud the sentences "I hate you" and "It was so funny" in the same voice—a wooden monotone. This was a problem. Her flat voice turned the best stories into the worst drone. Her colorless inflection took the meaning out of words. She couldn't understand the twists of plot or the feelings of the stories' characters.

Charlene needed to improve her reading comprehension. But perhaps she needed an acting lesson first. With this in mind, I greeted her one afternoon in a rather odd way.

"Oh, Charlene, I'm so happy today," I groaned in a pathetic voice.

"You don't sound happy," she said. "You sound sad."

"Then it worked. Hooray! It's a new game I was trying, called SAY IT WITH FEELING. In this game you say things with a lot of feeling, but you don't use the *right* feeling. You use the *wrong* feeling. That's why I said I was happy, but in an unhappy way. I wonder if I can say 'I'm so sad' but make it sound happy."

"I bet I can," Charlene piped in.

"Go ahead," I said.

"I'm so sad," she said. She nearly shrieked with joy. It was a fine performance.

"Here's another. Can you say 'Let's go play' and make it sound angry?" I asked.

With an earnest look, Charlene began. She sounded murderous. Another first-rate performance. We were ready, clearly, for some more difficult tasks. I asked her, therefore, to say, "Is that a polka-dotted zebra?"—but make the words sound scared. Then the same sentence, but make the words sound thrilled. Then the same polka-dotted zebra, but make the words snooty, as if she were too good for the likes of polka-dotted zebras. Charlene said the words, and her performances were flawless.

That was enough SAY IT WITH FEELING for one day, but it wasn't the last time we played. In fact, we began most every tutoring session with a bit of "feeling" talk. Charlene never got bored. She loved the ridiculousness of this game. I tried to keep things fun by making the sentences silly and the emotions strange.

A few weeks later, I interrupted Charlene as she was reading about an angry encounter between a bear and a frog.

"How do you think Bear feels when he tells Frog to go away and never come back?" I asked.

"He's angry," Charlene answered.

"Well, then, can you say 'Go away, Frog' in a furiously angry voice?" I asked.

Charlene could and did.

"That was great, Charlene. Your voice made me feel Bear's anger."

Charlene glowed with delight. This was a turning point. Over the next few months Charlene's reading voice transformed from monotone to multitone. Listening to her read was a delight. And, once she understood that words on the page express feelings and aren't just empty statements, reading seemed suddenly more interesting.

CIRCLE STORY

Melissa picked up her first book with regular chapters, read all the way through chapter one, and beamed with pride at what she had just done. I was proud of her too. Reading an entire chapter was a real achievement. But how well did she understand what she read? I was afraid to ask about the content because I didn't want Melissa to feel I was quizzing her. Instead I asked her to predict what would happen next. This was a sly question. Melissa could predict the story's future only if she understood its past. Asking her to predict had a second benefit too. It forced her to conceive a set of expectations about the story. A reader with expectations naturally pays closer attention to plot and character. You want to know: Will Sally go to the haunted house? Will George follow Sally? By making Melissa predict what would happen next, I was making her concentrate more closely on the story. Melissa wasn't always so good at predicting. To strengthen her skill, we played CIRCLE STORY, which was easy and fun.

What is a CIRCLE STORY? It's a tale that passes from one person to another, building as it goes. Here's the beginning of one created by Melissa and Peggy:

Peggy: Once upon a time, Chuck the chipmunk was walking in the woods when he saw an elf caught in a trap. Your turn, Melissa. What happens next?

Melissa: Chuck let the elf out of the trap.

Peggy: Good suggestion! The elf was very happy and he invited Chuck to his home for dinner. Your turn.

Melissa: The elf's home was underground.

Peggy: The elf made dinner in a special way. He wished for whatever he wanted.

Melissa: Chuck wished he could have magic like that.

Peggy: The elf wanted Chuck to be happy, and so he granted him one magic wish.

Melissa: Chuck thought and thought. Finally he decided on his wish . . .

What will Chuck's wish be? Perhaps he'll request a magic bowl, always full of acorns. Maybe he'll insist on a pair of wings, so that he can fly like a bird. Any addition that fits the plot and goes with the characters will do. Looking for a sensible story line, that's the goal of CIRCLE STORY. It's also the goal of young readers seeking to understand short stories and even long chapter books.

READING ALOUD

Reading aloud to your child is probably the best single thing you can do to turn your child into a good reader. Read picture books, chapter books, poetry, fiction, nonfiction. Read before bedtime, after school, before dinner. Don't stop reading aloud just because your child learns to do his own reading. Read aloud easy books that a child can reread on his own. Your child will love it, and you will love it too, especially when you consider these four reasons:

When you read aloud to your child, you create a model of good reading. Your child needs to hear fluent, expressive reading before he can become a fluent, expressive reader himself.

When you read aloud to your child, you end up spending a little time discussing the stories too. You'll have your opinion about why a character acts in a certain manner and your child may have a different idea, just like people coming out of the movies. Having a little discussion makes thinking about the meaning of books a part of everyday life.

Good authors write words we don't normally use in daily conversation. Your child will learn new words, therefore, while listening to you read, which is a good thing, even if the child runs around the house saying "quoth" and "slay."

When you read to your child, you keep his excitement about books at a peak. Excitement is crucial. It is the secret of learning.

In the Appendix you'll find a list of good books for reading aloud. Look for books that both you and your child will enjoy. Remember, if you're bored, the child will notice and your example will not be helpful.

What can you do if you have more than one child? Occasionally, you'll find books that are good for every child in your family. Then, you can all sit together and enjoy a single story. Don't count on this ideal situation, however. In general, children who are more than two years apart in age will be interested in different books. Therefore, you will probably have to arrange a different daily reading time for each child. This needn't be difficult. In fact, you don't have to spend more than ten minutes reading to a child.

Ten minutes is ample time to complete most picture books; ten minutes is also long enough to find out the next bit of action in a chapter book. So when two children are clamoring for their stories, you can say, "I will read to Jeffrey for ten minutes now, and then it will be Karen's turn. Karen, you can listen to Jeffrey's story if you want and if he agrees, or you can do something quiet like draw a picture until we're done." Of course, if you end up reading for a bit longer than ten minutes, well, that's okay too.

Should reading aloud replace other ten-minute games and activities? Absolutely not. Ideally, reading aloud to your child will join other daily rituals, like eating breakfast, brushing teeth, and making the bed. With reading aloud established as a regular part of each and every day, you'll still have plenty of time for other ten-minute activities.

chapter 6

The Writer's Trade

Evan loved to write. He wrote stories, poems, and chapter books. He wrote in notebooks, on scrap paper, on index cards, on the computer. He wrote in pencil, crayon, and pen. Evan couldn't get enough of it.

Judy hated writing. She had trouble forming letters. She fretted over spelling. She couldn't think of anything to say, or else she had so much to say she couldn't possibly get all the words down on paper. Writing was a headache.

When I worked with Evan, I didn't need to encourage him to write, but I did want to provide him with writing projects that would expand his imagination and train him to write clearly and distinctly. Judy, on the other hand, needed lots of encouragement. For Judy, I needed ideas to make writing fun instead of frustrating and scary.

Strangely enough, writing projects that expanded Evan's imagination usually interested Judy as well. What's more, writing ideas that were fun for Judy often pleased Evan too. Of course, the final results were different for Evan and Judy. Evan wrote with ease. The words in his head drifted effortlessly down to the page. He had a natural grace with language.

Judy had to struggle. Her ideas were often confused, her stories hard to understand. Still, with practice, Judy learned to hold ideas in her head until her hand could get the letters on the paper. She even began to relax a little, and as she relaxed, her stories became better organized and easier to follow.

In this chapter, you will find five activities that succeeded beautifully with both Evan and Judy. One or another should prove fun and helpful for your child as well. You will also find two activities designed to help your child's spelling improve.

Barbara wrote "The Magic Flower" when she was in first grade. The tale had charm and suspense from the very beginning:

> Once upon a time, a little girl had a special flower. The flower could talk and it told the girl how to make magic.

"The Magic Flower" eventually became five pages long, which, for a first-grader, is practically *War and Peace*. Barbara made up the adventure herself, but she didn't write it down. Instead, I acted as a secretary, recording her every word. When Barbara finished telling the story, I gave her a chance to make changes and corrections as she saw fit. Our work wasn't accomplished in one sitting. Instead, Barbara composed "The Magic Flower" in ten-minute spurts over the course of several weeks.

"The Magic Flower" was one of many tales Barbara spun over months of tutoring. When she finished dictating a story, she usually wanted to turn her pages into a book. This was easy enough to do, if I kept three things in mind while recording her words. First, I wrote on only one side of the paper. Second, I left a four-inch blank space on the top of each page. When the story was finished, Barbara could use this space to draw illustrations, and, because the reverse side of the paper was blank, she could use markers without worrying about the ink bleeding through. Third, I made sure there was a one-inch margin on the left side of each page.

GRADES

kindergarten, first, second, and third

MATERIALS

paper
pencil
optional: stapler
construction paper
plastic folder
colored markers

With things set up this way, book publishing was a snap. We simply stapled Barbara's pages together between sheets of colorful construction paper. Barbara drew a picture, wrote the title on the cover, and we were done.

When Barbara wanted a fancier production job, we did things a little differently. First she designed a title page for the story, complete with illustration. Then I went to the stationery store and bought a see-through plastic folder, the kind that comes with a plastic rib. We stapled her cover and story together inside the plastic folder. Next we slid the rib over the staples, and we oohed and aahed over our handiwork. Oohing and aahing was definitely a part of the activity.

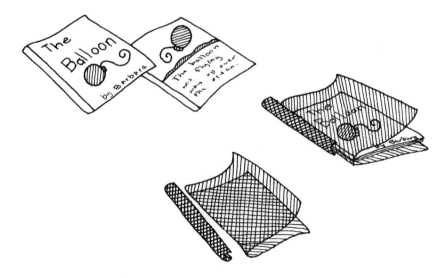

When should children give up dictating and start writing for themselves? As soon as they want to. A little encouragement from Mom and Dad might hasten the day. In fact, with encouragement, even very young writers can jot a few words on paper. The child won't employ standard spelling. Often very young writers won't put down more than a letter or even a scribble for each word. That's okay. Getting anything at all on the page is good preparation for more sophisticated writing to come.

On the other hand, once your child is writing on his own, should you stop taking dictation? Not necessarily. I've taken dictation from sixth-graders and found that it was good for them now and then. Writing without having to worry about penmanship, spelling, and punctuation can excite and liberate older writers. So mix things up: sometimes take dictation, sometimes encourage your child to write for himself.

Before you know it, you'll have a finished story. Now take out the stapler, the markers, the title page—and presto, a major opus. Ooh! Aah!

TEN-MINUTE WRITING

GRADES

first, second, and third

MATERIALS

paper
pencil

For Gregory, writing meant nothing but misery. He'd do anything to avoid it—tell jokes, drop pencils, even offer to *read*. Gregory would feel better about writing once he became a better writer. But how to become a better writer? Only by writing—catch-22.

Gregory and I struck a deal. He would write for merely ten minutes during our work sessions, never a second more, never a second less. And further, I wouldn't watch him do it. Instead, I too would write during those few minutes. Gregory liked this. He liked seeing me cross out words, make mistakes, change my mind, compose with messy handwriting, and even misspell a word or two. My errors reassured him. He had never seen the messy first drafts that writers know so well. He'd only seen finished editions—printed pages in books and magazines that didn't look a bit like his sloppy handwritten drafts. The discrepancy disturbed him. But when he saw that my own first efforts weren't much neater than his, he relaxed.

At the beginning of our ten minutes, we picked a topic. Sometimes we wrote stories. Sometimes we composed lists: three ways to make a teacher mad, five good meals for a vampire, six ways to make your mother laugh, and the like. Then we wrote for ten minutes, he on his composition and I on mine. Finally, we read our work to each other. If one of us didn't finish a story or a list, we could either continue with it during our next writing time or leave it undone in favor of a new theme.

I invented this system for Gregory, but I've used it successfully with other children—children who normally hate to write as well as children who love writing. If you want to give it a try, here are a few things you can do to make writing more attractive. Buy two fine-looking notebooks and declare them your writing journals. Get some impressive pencils to use in your journals. Colorful stickers decorating the cover and the pages might be a nice touch. Pick unharried times for writing. Such moments are rare in today's world, so when you can arrange for them, take advantage. Your child may want to spend more than ten minutes writing. If that's okay with you, go ahead. Ten minutes, though, is perfectly sufficient for a child to become more accustomed to writing.

You will, of course, need interesting topics for TEN-MINUTE WRITING. Here is a list of ten TEN-MINUTE ideas to get you started:

The Day I Was Invisible
The Meanest Person in the World
The War Between *Tyrannosaurus Rex* and Triceratops
Eight Things to Pack for a Trip to the Moon
The Day I Was Very, Very Angry
What I'd Buy with One Million Dollars
My Perfect Birthday
Five Ways to Trick an Evil Witch
My Advice to First-Graders (or Second-Graders, or Third-Graders)
Four Things I'd Do Differently if I Were My Mother (or Father, or Child, or Teacher)

What if your child hates everything about TEN-MINUTE WRITING? What if he's indifferent to fancy notebooks, despises stickers, thinks the stories and lists are stupid, and feels that writing with you means that the agonies of school have followed him home? What should you do? Put TEN-MINUTE WRITING aside. Maybe next month, or next year, he'll give the activity another chance. What a difference a year can make. Meanwhile, how about a JOKE BOOK?

JOKE BOOK

GRADES

first, second, and third

MATERIALS

paper
pencil
staples
construction paper
optional: a joke book

Carl wasn't keen on writing. Every story-writing project we started produced whines, complaints, protests of boredom. Exasperated, I finally said, "Come on, Carl, there must be *something* you'd like to write."

He realized I was annoyed, so he took my question seriously. After a moment's thought, he replied, "How about jokes? Can I write one of my favorites?"

Now I had to think. Would writing a joke achieve the goals I had in mind? Clearly, if Carl was retelling jokes he wasn't making up the story himself. But he would have to concentrate on other aspects of writing. He'd have to say the words to himself slowly enough to write them down one by one. That's a difficult aspect of writing for many youngsters, harder than for adults. Children think much faster than they write; they have trouble holding a string of words in mind for the time it takes to record the words on paper. Carl would also have to cope with penmanship and spelling too. So I told him to go ahead.

He bent over the paper. When he was done, his page looked like this:

How du you no a banand is
poplr
It has a peel

Sure, there were mistakes. But he and I could both read the riddle. I laughed; it was a success. What's more, Carl actually asked to write a second joke. I'm not sure which of us was more startled by this request.

My answer, however, was no. I suggested instead that we begin our next tutoring session with joke writing. Carl would write a new joke while I typed a polished draft of his banana-appeal riddle. I pointed out that if we began each tutoring session this way, soon

enough we'd have a large anthology of typed funnies. Eventually
we could illustrate the jokes,

staple the pages together with a construction-paper cover,

and have a book: *Carl's Favorite Jokes.*

This sounded fine to Carl, and at our next tutoring session we began our joke workshop. Carl wrote a new favorite joke; I typed up the banana riddle. Session after session, going one joke at a time, one joke per sheet of paper, we eventually collected a thick manuscript: fifteen pages. Carl was proud of himself. He never thought he could write so much. It was such an accomplishment, in fact, that we decided to make seven copies of the book. That way, I could keep one and Carl could distribute the others to friends, family, and teachers. It was easy enough to produce this limited edition. We photocopied each page, made enough construction-paper covers to go around, and stapled the books together.

You and your child can make a joke book at home following the same method. If you don't like typing, you can copy the jokes carefully by hand. If your child prefers, he can do the rough draft and the final draft too.

What happens if your child runs out of jokes? You might poke around in a children's joke book—you'll find some titles in the Appendix under *Books for Reading Aloud*. Even taking several minutes for research, your child should still be able to write down a joke in about ten minutes. Just be sure not to worry about the errors. Perhaps you'd like to start with Carl's second joke:

Q: What's the best thing to put in a pie?
A: Your teeth.

I give it ten laugh points.

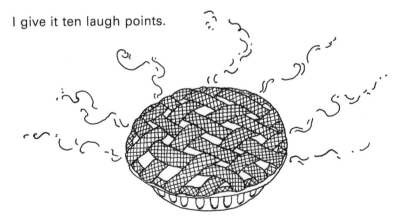

One Monday morning, Ryan strolled into my workroom and greeted me with a good-natured hello. I didn't answer back. Instead, I handed her a piece of paper that read:

GRADES

second and third

MATERIALS

paper
pencil

No talking allowed for 10 minutes.

"What do you mean?" she asked.

"I'll explain. But after the explanation, no talking aloud allowed. We're going to have a SILENT CONVERSATION. In SILENT CONVERSATION, you write everything you want to say. No talking permitted. Well, certain talking is okay. If I write a word you can't read, you can point to the word and I'll read it for you. If you write a word I can't read, I'll point and you'll read for me. Spelling doesn't count, but if you want to spell a word correctly, you can ask me the word and I'll write it on a piece of scrap paper. That's the idea. Are you ready to start silent talking?"

Ryan solemnly nodded her head. I began to write.

How was your weekend?

Did anything special happen?

Ryan took the pencil out of my hand and wrote:

I went to see a movee

Now it was my turn.

What movie did you see?

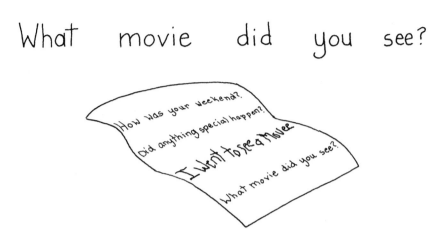

Ryan had seen a Walt Disney classic. She'd gone to a Chinese restaurant and eaten chicken with orange flavor. By the time Ryan told me all of this, our ten minutes of SILENT CONVERSATION were up. Ryan was disappointed. She liked this odd and challenging method of communication. She liked it so much, we got in the habit of starting each tutoring session with a ten-minute SILENT CONVERSATION. In the course of our "talk," I discovered Ryan's favorite rock star (Michael Jackson), her least favorite TV show (*Mister Rogers' Neighborhood*), the top item on her Christmas list (a new pair of ice skates), and her younger brother's annoying habit of blaming her for *everything*.

You and your child might like conversing silently. You won't know until you try. When's a good time? How about before a bedtime story, or after lunch on a rainy day? How about while waiting for pizza to be delivered, or while traveling on a train? Make sure the moment seems appropriate to both you and your child. If things turn sour—if writing seems stressful rather than playful—the activity won't serve its purpose. But if you do have fun, then SILENT CONVERSATION (Quiet, everyone—writers at work) may be here to stay.

The first time I tried SILENT CONVERSATION with Tony, it flopped. Tony had nothing to say. He was unwilling to write about his life in or out of school. I wasn't about to torture him with a detested writing assignment, but I did want him to spend a few minutes writing. How?

"Here's an idea," I said. "Instead of silent talking for ten minutes, let's work together on a story. First I'll write a little. Then you'll write a little. Then I'll write again, until we finish." A glimmer of interest shone in Tony's eyes, so I started to write.

GRADES

second and third

MATERIALS

paper
pencil

On Fred's way home from school, he met a man from outer space. The man from space grabbed Fred and took him off to a waiting spaceship

I handed the pencil to Tony. "It's your turn. You think of what happens now. You don't need to tell too much. Just the next little bit. Then it will be my turn again."

"I don't know what to say," Tony grumbled.

"You could describe the spaceship. I'm curious to know what it was like. You could tell about the space people. What do they look like? Are they good guys or bad guys? What do they want with Fred? Do they have special powers?"

"I have an idea," he said. He picked up a pencil. Before writing he asked, "Does spelling count?"

"No," I answered. "Spelling never counts when you're getting your ideas down on the paper. Later, if we like the story, we can work on spelling, punctuation, and other such details."

Tony was ready. He started to write.

The spasmen had pwrs
and culd be invsble

My turn again.

Because the men were invisible
Fred couldn't see them, but he
could hear them talking. The space
people spoke space language, but
somehow Fred understood every word.

Tony's turn again. Another few rounds of writing and our ten minutes was up. Much to Tony's surprise, he'd had fun writing. He didn't even object when I told him that we'd continue Fred's adventures at the beginning of our next tutoring session. In fact, it took us several ten-minute writing sessions to tell how Fred saved the world from alien invasion. It was a great story, and was followed some weeks later by its sequel: "Fred Meets the Underwater Monster."

When a child is busy putting ideas down on paper, spelling shouldn't be an important consideration. Writing words, even misspelled words, is accomplishment enough. Spelling is important, however, and with a little help from you, your child will find it easier and easier to do it with dictionary precision. In fact, if you played the games in Chapter 4: Sounds Abound or the games in Chapter 3: Word Power, you were actually helping your child with spelling at the same time you helped him with reading. But here are two games, BODY WRITING and ERASER, designed specifically for this purpose.

Begin BODY WRITING by thinking of a simple word, like *jump*. Don't tell your child the word. Instead, trace the word on the back of your child's hand while his eyes are closed. Start with the *j* and keep tracing until your child knows for sure that *j* is the first letter in your word. Then start the *u.* Next trace the *m.* Meanwhile your child is busy thinking what words begin with *j*, *ju*, *jum*. His mind acts like a dictionary. He filters through lists of words. He uses letter sounds. He creates a picture of the word. Successful spellers do exactly these things. They listen to the letter sounds. They create mental pictures of the words they want to spell. BODY WRITING gives your child an opportunity to practice these skills in playful (and occasionally ticklish) ways. If the child figures out the word before you finish spelling, he should get an extra hip-hip-hooray. If it takes all the letters before he figures out the word, he should still get a big cheer. If he can't figure out the word, tell him not to worry. BODY WRITING is a hard game; no one can be expected to get every word. Just go on to a new round, making sure to pick a word that is easier to decipher.

This time, though, you might write on the child's palm, forearm, or back. Your child will undoubtedly want a turn to out-spell you too. Go ahead, let him. He can use words he knows how to spell by heart or look in a book, magazine, or the dictionary for a less familiar word. Play a few rounds and then stop. It's best, in fact, to stop while the game is still exciting. That way, the child will be eager to play again in a few days or a few weeks.

BODY WRITING

GRADES

first and second

ERASER

GRADES

second and third

MATERIALS

paper
pencil
eraser

Some children learn to spell by listening to every sound in a word and matching the sounds with letters. These children spell the way they hear, sound by sound. Other children are more visual in their approach. Say a word to these children and they make a mental image of how it looks, letter by letter. They see the word in their mind's eye and then write what they see. Though either approach is good, neither is sufficient. The best spellers combine both. These children take advantage of the phonetic elements in English, but they aren't thrown by the words that don't follow phonetic rules. Their visual memory of words helps them write a word like *said*, which sounds different from the curious way it's spelled.

Jack, a second-grader, didn't possess this visual ability. He relied entirely on sounds to spell words. When words were spelled peculiarly, Jack was at a loss. Could a game help? ERASER could, and did.

ERASER is a variation on an old-time game, Hangman. In Hangman, you think of a mystery word and draw dashes on a page to represent the number of letters in your word. Then your child guesses letters he thinks are in the word. When the child guesses correctly, you write the letter in the proper spot. When the child makes a mistake, you draw a bit of a person ready to dangle from a hangman's gallows. If your child discovers your word before you finish drawing a complete hanged man, he wins the game.

z e b r a

If you hang the man before the child gets the word, you win.

Hangman is a good game: it helps children develop skills in spelling, and it's fun. Younger children, however, often find the game difficult and frustrating instead of enjoyable. This was the case with Jack. ERASER is a simpler alternative. It was just right for Jack.

Before the game began, I wrote the entire alphabet on a sheet of paper. I also drew a stick figure named Eraserman.

a b c d e f
g h i j k l
m n o p q r
s t u v w x
y z

Then I picked a word for our game: *elephant*. In regular Hangman, I would then draw eight dashes on the paper to represent the eight letters in the word *elephant*. In ERASER, I did something a little different. I drew letter frames for the eight letters. The frames show the shape of the letters. The short letters—*e*, *a*, and *n*—got squares: ☐. The long letters that stretched up—*l*, *h*, and *t*—got rectangles that stretched up: ▯; the *p*, which stretched down, got a rectangle that stretched down: ▯. The frames gave Jack hints about the

letters in the word. When he looked at the alphabet, he could use the letter frames as a guide. This made it easier for him to figure out the mystery word. It also gave him a strong visual reference for the word. Here is *elephant*:

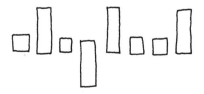

Turning *elephant* into a visual picture was my goal in this game. I wanted Jack to think about how words looked and not rely exclusively on sounds.

Every time Jack guessed a letter correctly, I wrote it in the appropriate frame. When Jack erred, I erased part of the stick figure. Whether Jack guessed correctly or incorrectly, I crossed that letter out of the alphabet. Jack began by guessing *e*. That was a fine guess—*elephant* has two *e*'s, so I had to fill in two frames. I also crossed out the *e* from the alphabet.

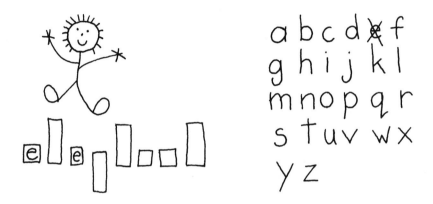

Next he guessed *u*. That wasn't such a lucky choice. I erased the hair of Eraserman and crossed out the *u* in the alphabet.

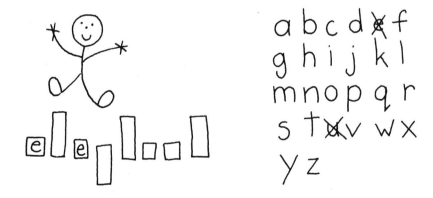

Then Jack guessed a third letter, and a fourth, and a fifth. His goal was to fill in all the frames with letters before I erased all of Eraserman. If he could do it, he'd win the game. If he couldn't, he'd lose.

ERASER is simple to learn, simple to play, takes less than ten minutes, and it's very effective.

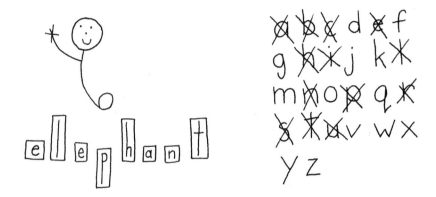

PART THREE
COUNTING ON MATH

chapter 7

Counting and Beyond

Preschoolers chant, "One, two, three, four"—and with these mesmerizing words they enter the world of numbers. An average child, by the start of kindergarten, can count a little past ten. Knowledge and skills mushroom after that. By the end of first grade, children are ideally able to count, read, and write from one to a hundred. By the end of third grade, children are expected to count, read, and write into the thousands. They should be able to start counting from numbers other than one; count backwards from a higher number to a lower one; and count by fives, tens, fours, and threes.

Reciting numbers in the right order is crucial—but it's only a beginning. Numbers must be more than mere words, they must signify quantities. Most adults assume that children automatically link the word *seven* with the quantity of seven. Not so! Children may memorize the word *seven* and may remember that it comes after the word *six* and before *eight*. But they may not understand the meaning of seven. Watch a young child count seven pretzels and you'll see that linking quantity with words is not an easy thing. The child is likely to say two numbers for a single pretzel or skip saying a number for one of the pretzels. He may get a total of eight pretzels, or perhaps six—but not seven.

Six of the games in this chapter, COUNTING ALL THE TIME, HAND CLAPS, MAGAZINE COUNTING, HUNT FOR NUMBERS, COUNTING CONTESTS, and DO IT BEFORE I COUNT TO . . . will spruce up anyone's counting and understanding of number. Children will play while they set the dinner table, clean their rooms, and hop across the kitchen floor.

As children get older, they must develop even more sophisticated notions of quantity. For instance, how many pennies can you fit in a paper cup? Unless you count, you can't know the exact amount. Still, you do know that three is too little and three hundred too much. The better your quantitative judgment, the closer your estimate. Someone with a terrific sense of numbers may be able to approximate the needed pennies within a range of ten or twenty. With practice, even first-, second-, and third-graders can learn to estimate with such striking precision. That's the goal of the next two games, ESTIMATE IT and HOW CLOSE CAN YOU GET?

In the first years of school, children must take yet another step. They must understand how the number system works. They must confront the number system head on. Take the number thirty-four. Sometime in first grade, your child will discover that although thirty-four indicates thirty-four individual numbers, it also indicates three groups of ten and four ones. This understanding requires two concepts. Your child must appreciate that the same symbol 3 stands for three ones in 53 but three tens in 34, because of the difference in place. Place value is the name of this concept.

Second, your child must understand that in our number system we organize numbers into groups of ten. The 3 in 34 indicates three tens—not three eights or three sixes. Ten groups of ten make a hundred. The 3 in 375, therefore, represents three hundreds, or three sets of ten groups of ten. These are difficult ideas to understand, even for adults. Playing three games in this chapter, HOW CLOSE CAN YOU GET?, COLLECT TEN, and TARGET, will make these ideas easier to understand for your child—and perhaps for you too.

Sometime in the middle of second grade, your child will discover that numbers can be rearranged. For instance, 56, which represents five groups of ten and six ones, can be rearranged into four groups of tens and sixteen ones. Why learn to rearrange numbers? Rearranging numbers is the actual procedure used for "borrowing" when you subtract and "carrying" when you add. A simple game, THE REARRANGE CONNECTION, can help your child master this not-so-simple mathematical notion.

Which games should you play? You should take notice of the suggested grade levels. Don't rush your child. A game that is fun and helpful for a third-grader will only confuse and irritate a first-grader, which will do more harm than good. Remember, though, that playing a first-grade game with a second- or third-grader is often the best way to illuminate never-before-understood ideas and thus get the youngster clicking with math as never before.

COUNTING ALL THE TIME

Counting is the seed from which all mathematics sprouts. To make the root healthy and strong, it's wise to encourage your kindergartener and first-grader to count a little bit every day. This is easy enough to do—and fun too. You can start tonight after dinner. Simply ask your child to count the number of doors in your house and report back to you. Tomorrow before lunch ask him to count how many shoes are in his closet. Once you get into the swing of it, you'll find something for your child to count almost anywhere, almost anytime. Soon you won't even think about it. It will be as natural to ask your child how many buttons are on his favorite shirt as it is to ask him to wash his hands before dinner.

To help you get going, here's a list of things to count:

dishes on the dinner table
spoons in the kitchen drawer
cookies on a plate
stuffed animals on the child's bed
towels in the bathroom
plants in the living room
pencils on the desk
books on a shelf
toes at the dinner table
peanuts in a bowl
ice cubes in a tray

Don't forget to count during car rides. Keep a special eye out for:

billboards
blue cars
antique stores
cars with dogs

Scenery speeds by. Numbers mount up. Your child spies thirty-one bicycle riders before you reach the beach—a fine day for counting.

Nina had just finished a painting and we were cleaning up the mess. Or rather, I was cleaning. She was humming and clapping. Clapping wasn't cleaning, but maybe it offered a good way to get Nina to practice counting.

I put down my sponge and said, "Your clapping reminds me of a game called HAND CLAPS. Here's how to play. I clap and you try to count my claps."

This sounded simple enough, and a lot better than cleanup, so she agreed to try. I clapped slowly four times. I expected Nina to count along with me, but that's not what happened. Instead, she waited until I finished, then she reproduced my claps. That's when she started to count. Why did Nina proceed this way? She thought it was necessary to know the whole amount before starting to count. Nina didn't realize that she could count as I clapped, and that her last number would be identical to the total number of claps.

Young children don't always understand that the last counting number plays a dual role. It is the last number counted *and* it tells about the total amount of objects counted. HAND CLAPS helped Nina develop this sophisticated notion of numbers.

We switched roles. She clapped, and I counted out loud. She clapped once, and I said, "One." Clap—"two." Clap—"three." Clap—"four." We did this a few times, then went back to my clapping and her counting. Gradually Nina noticed the difference between my approach and hers. After a few more rounds, she began to experiment with my way of counting. Eventually she caught on and always counted while I clapped.

Let me emphasize one point: I didn't teach Nina a new way to count claps. Instead, I created a model of counting that Nina could follow. As soon as she understood my technique, she took it up. I didn't need to say a word. All I needed was patience.

I stayed with small numbers until Nina could count as I clapped. Eight claps were plenty. Then I increased the number. Twenty is a reasonable top limit for this game. No matter how many times I clapped I always tried to go slow and leave a moment between each clap.

Clap, clap, clap.

HAND CLAPS

MAGAZINE COUNTING

GRADES

kindergarten, first, and second

MATERIALS

magazines

Does your child get the fidgets waiting in a doctor's office or sitting in a train station? Here's a way to fidget profitably. Pick up a magazine with lots of pictures. Your child thumbs through until he finds a picture he likes—a baby-food ad, for instance. Then you ask number questions about the picture. How many flowers are on the baby's blanket? How many buttons are on the father's shirt? How many fingers can you see? How many letters are in the word *peaches*? How many jars do you see? How many people are in the picture? How many spoons are in the picture? When you finish with one picture, turn to another. This time let your child ask the questions and you do the counting.

Once your child knows the game, you can try a tricky counting variation. Look at a clothing ad and ask, If we draw a hat on every head, how many hats will we draw? If you give each person two cookies, how many cookies will that be? How many flowers do you need to put three in every hand? It takes effort and number savvy to answer questions like these. Some children will enjoy the extra effort; others won't. After a question or two, you'll know if playing this way appeals to your child. If it doesn't, go back to the more straightforward number questions.

The numbers involved in MAGAZINE COUNTING are usually small. But not always. Once I counted sixty-three raisins while looking at a cereal ad. Getting kids to count to high figures like sixty-three is a good way to help them practice saying their numbers—and will keep them from fidgeting too.

HUNT FOR NUMBERS

Many children count very well but have trouble reading and writing the numbers. That was Hillary's problem. She could count to one hundred, but she confused the written symbols. She mistook 51 for 15 and wrote 34 as 304. HUNT FOR NUMBERS was just the game to help Hillary with this problem.

In the middle of a tutoring session one afternoon, I challenged Hillary to find the number 12 in my office. I wrote 12 down on a piece of paper to help her out. She looked high and low, until she spotted the 12 on my wall clock.

"I found it!" she squealed.

"Bravo," I said. "Would you care to hunt for a new number?"

"Sure. That was fun," she answered.

I had her look for 27 (she found it on a calendar) and 31 (on the TV dial), then 75 (with some hints from me, she found it on the top of a light bulb). Next, I let her send me on a number hunt. I told her I was willing to look for any number between 1 and 100. She came up with 64. With a little assistance, she wrote the number on a piece of paper for me to use in the hunt. I searched and searched. I checked food cans and a tissue box, the radio dial and numbers on colored pencils. Finally, as a last resort, I opened a book to page 64. Hillary and I agreed that looking in books was sort of cheating, but that once in a while, when all else failed, cheating would have to do.

Hillary loved this game. She was eager to play again and again, which was fine with me. Besides helping her read and write numbers, hunting served a second function. It proved to Hillary that numbers are everywhere. She was often surprised at the peculiar places numbers appear: in shoes, on notebook covers, on clothes, on paper-clip boxes, on perfume bottles. No wonder math is such an important subject!

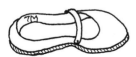

DO IT BEFORE
I COUNT
TO . . .

Orders, orders, orders. You'd think children would rebel.

> Wash your hands before I count from one to twenty.
> Put on your gloves before I count from seventy-five to ninety.
> Finish your peas before I count backwards from sixty to twenty-five.
> Comb your hair before I count by tens to two hundred.
> Button your coat before I count by fives from one hundred to two hundred.

But children are delighted to obey when I accompany orders with a numerical challenge, DO IT BEFORE I COUNT TO . . . I always vary my manner of counting. Sometimes I begin with the number one, other times with one hundred. I count forward and backwards. I count by ones or skip count by fives, tens, threes, or eights. And children love it. Before long they try to sing along with my counting swirls and leaps. They, too, count high numbers, count backwards, and skip count.

Sometimes, when I have no special orders to be obeyed, I ask a child to do silly things, like tiptoe across the room before I count by threes from one to thirty, or walk around the table before I count from 1,000 to 1,030. The child does it for fun, and along the way picks up some fancy counting. What could be better?

*D*avid, a second-grader, was good at counting—as long as the numbers went forward. If you asked him to count backwards, he had a hard time. He managed the blast-off chant: ten, nine, eight . . . But if you asked him to count backwards from twenty, he had to first count *forward* to twenty before he could shift gears and say nineteen. Then he would count forward to nineteen, shift gears, and say eighteen. He continued in this seesaw fashion until he reached ten and could do the blast-off chant.

This was no good. He could hardly go forward in arithmetic if he couldn't count back from twenty. How could I help him? I could lecture. I could insist he recite numbers over and over. Or I could play COUNTING CONTESTS with him.

"David," I said before our first competition, "I challenge you to a who-can-say-hippopotamus-the-most contest. I bet I can say more hippopotamuses while you count from twenty to eight than you can say hippopotamuses while I count the same numbers. How about it? Do you want to try and out-hippo me?"

"Okay," said David.

I took a piece of paper and wrote the numbers zero to twenty. I knew David could read these numbers perfectly well even though he couldn't manage a backwards count from memory. (If your child can't read the numbers yet, you'll have to wait before playing this game.) I explained to David that he needed to find twenty on the numbered strip and then he could read each number down to eight.

"While you count," I said, "I'll say 'hippopotamus' over and over. Every time I say 'hippopotamus,' I'll put a check on a paper scorecard. When you finish counting, I'll stop saying 'hippopotamus' and we'll switch roles. I'll count while *you* say 'hippopotamus' and

GRADES

kindergarten and first

MATERIALS

paper
pencil
scissors
tape
various items for counting

record *your* hippos with check marks on your own scorecard. Then we'll see who has the most checks."

"I think I get it," said David. "Let's go. Ready?"

I was ready. Not ready enough to beat David, however. He won, twenty-four hippos to eighteen. Of course, he liked winning, but I think he also liked hearing me say my hippopotamuses. There has to be a fun part, after all.

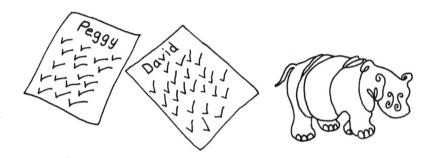

For our second contest, I bet I could tiptoe farther than David during a nineteen-to-eleven count. To keep track of our steps, we marked the starting line and our different stopping points with masking tape. Our third contest was also a tiptoe contest, but the count was from forty-two to thirty-three. To help David count in this contest, I gave him a new piece of paper with the numbers thirty through fifty.

Gradually, David felt more at ease counting backwards. Then, and only then, I took away the numbered strips. That was risky. I wanted him to learn, but I didn't want to frustrate him. If he lost too many contests, he would surely get frustrated. So I gave him a handicap. I told him that since it was harder for him to count without seeing the numbers, we needed to do something to keep the contests fair. I suggested that I'd always say five more numbers than he'd say. If he counted from twenty to thirteen, I'd count from twenty-five to thirteen. If he counted from thirteen to zero, I'd count from eighteen to zero. David thought this was a fine idea, and so all was well.

David and I competed with each other several times a week. It took a certain effort on my part to come up with good contests. Not all competitions turned out well. Here are some that worked for David and me. You and your child might want to begin your COUNTING CONTESTS with them:

How many coins can you toss into a hat while I count from twenty to four?

How many times can you write your name while I count from fifty to thirty-five?

How many numbers can you write starting at one and counting forward while I count backwards from thirty-two to eleven?

How far can you walk backwards while I count from one hundred to eighty?

How many times can you clap (and count your own claps) while I count from sixty-six to fifty?

ESTIMATE IT

GRADES

first, second, and third

MATERIALS

various items for counting

*B*urt knew what to expect when he entered my office. The first task of the hour was always the same.

"What am I estimating today?" he asked.

"Peanuts," I said. "Here's a bowl. You can eat them, but first you have to estimate how many there are. Then we'll count them—not eating yet—and see how close the estimate was. Now remember—"

"I know," he interrupted. "An estimate isn't supposed to be exact. That's for counting. An estimate is supposed to be sensible."

He was quoting me because he'd heard me say these lines so often.

Burt knew the ESTIMATE IT rules. He could pick up the bowl and tilt it or shake it. He could count the top layer of nuts—by eye, but not with his finger. Whatever method he used, however, he had to have his estimate ready in one minute. My wristwatch was the official timekeeper. After sixty seconds, Burt declared his estimate and the formal count began.

Why start Burt's tutoring sessions like this? Burt was in third grade and completely befuddled by his math work in school. The root of his problem wasn't hard to see. He lacked an accurate sense of numbers. If you asked him to solve a problem like 17 + 11, he might come up with 52 or 16—it was all the same to him. The numbers held no meaning for him.

His first estimates, when confronted by a bowl of nuts or a handful of pennies, were wild. How many pennies? Twenty-four, or maybe a hundred, or perhaps a thousand—who could tell? After just a few tries, he began to narrow in, though. How many books on the shelf? Maybe fifty or eighty. His estimates became even more refined. How many kidney beans can fit in a tablespoon? About thirty-five. How many books could he balance on his head? Around five. How many raisins in a box? Maybe 150.

Burt's skill in estimation developed because he checked each estimate against an actual count. By comparing his count and his estimate, he was forced to take his estimates seriously, to put some thought into them, to consider what a number might mean.

Often, halfway through counting, Burt realized his estimate was way off. He'd get discouraged. When this happened, I gave him the opportunity to revise his estimates. This brightened his spirits and gave him a second chance to strengthen his grasp on numbers.

Sometimes, when we had large amounts to count—150 raisins, for instance—we didn't go one by one. We made little raisin piles instead. Each pile held ten raisins. Then we counted ten by ten. This system made counting large numbers easier, and at the same time gave Burt a little practice in the system of grouping by tens. That's the basis of our number system, so a little practice was a good idea.

Estimating and counting can help all children—even topflight math students—enrich their understanding of numbers. What should you estimate at home? Anything and everything: the spoons in a kitchen drawer, the grapes on a stem, the pages in a book, the M&M's in a bag, the pencils that can fit in a glass, the dried beans tnat can fill a spoon, the leaves on a plant, the jelly beans you can hold in your hand.

One more thing: your child may like the game better if you too take your turn at estimating. So go ahead and test your number awareness against your child's. Sure, you'll make mistakes. But your errors may have a good effect on your child. When the child sees that mistakes don't bother you, he'll relax and feel comfortable about his misestimations.

Burt guessed there were fifty peanuts in the bowl. I guessed forty. There were actually only twenty. Still, good enough. When you play with peanuts, all answers are winning answers. And the prize? A peanut snack, in this case.

HOW CLOSE CAN YOU GET?

On one of her first visits to me, Amanda said: "Fifty-six means five groups of ten and six ones. Twenty-four means two groups of ten and four ones." That was impressive. She appeared to have a firm grasp on that great mathematical mystery, place value.

Oddly, though, Amanda's knowledge of place value consisted of knowing the right words to say, but the words were devoid of meaning for her. She knew how to chant a formula, the way someone might chant Einstein's $E = mc^2$ without understanding anything about Einstein, energy, mass, the speed of light, or squared numbers.

So there was a problem: How to help Amanda endow her words with mathematical meaning? One game did the trick: HOW CLOSE CAN YOU GET?

I gathered the necessary equipment: a piece of paper, a pencil, a bowl of dried kidney beans, and ten small paper cups. Then I picked a number. Not just any number; only a multiple of ten would do—ten, twenty, thirty, forty, fifty, sixty, seventy, eighty, ninety, or one hundred. For our initial game, I chose thirty. Then I challenged Amanda to dip her hand into the bowl and try to gather exactly thirty beans. She could fiddle with the beans as long as she liked. She could take more beans from the bowl or return a few. She could spread the beans out on the table. But she couldn't count them. She had to estimate the number.

When she was satisfied with her estimation, we started counting. As we counted the beans we placed them in the paper cups—ten beans per cup.

In this case, since Amanda was aiming for thirty beans, we set out three cups. Three cups—ten beans in each cup, three groups of ten—that's thirty. If she estimated perfectly, if she picked exactly thirty beans, she'd fill each cup with ten beans and have no beans left over. Such ideal results were exceedingly rare. In general, she either had an excess of beans after filling the cups or needed additional ones to finish the job. If she had beans left over, we counted the extras for her score. Or, alternatively, if she lacked beans, we counted how many beans were missing, and that was her score. Either way, she wrote her score on a piece of paper so we wouldn't forget it.

Then the beans went back into the bowl and it was my turn. I dipped my hand into the bowl and pulled out what I hoped were thirty beans. Like Amanda, I could mull over my estimate as long as I wanted. I could fiddle with the beans as much as I liked. But I couldn't count them. When I felt confident about my pile, I began filling the three paper cups. I hoped to have ten beans in each cup and no extras. My score was, like Amanda's, determined by the number of extra beans I had after filling the cups or the number of additional beans I needed to make thirty. In this game, the player with the lowest score wins.

How did this game help Amanda? Every time I picked a multiple of ten, Amanda had to figure out how many paper cups we needed.

Initially, she counted by tens: "Thirty beans means we need one cup for ten, two cups for twenty, three cups for thirty." She did the same for sixty beans, discovering we needed six cups. And then for twenty beans, realizing we needed two cups. She noted a pattern: thirty—three cups; sixty—six cups; twenty—two cups. "I get it," she shouted. "Each cup gets ten beans, so fifty will be five cups because fifty is five tens!" The words made sense. It was a grand moment in Amanda's mathematical career. Her understanding was confirmed on the next round when it turned out she'd overestimated by twenty-three beans. "I could have filled up two more cups," she said. "And I'd still have three beans left." A superb insight, a fine day.

Sometimes Amanda needed help computing her score, not when she had too many beans but when she had too few. Once, when aiming for seventy, she ran out of beans after filling four cups with ten beans and a fifth cup with a mere three beans.

To figure out her score, we first considered the two completely empty cups. Amanda could see that to fill these cups she needed twenty beans. Then we looked at the partially filled cup. With a little help, Amanda determined that she needed seven beans to finish filling it up. Twenty, and seven more. That was her score: twenty-seven.

Amanda and I played HOW CLOSE CAN YOU GET? often over the course of the next several months. It only took ten minutes of our time to play a round or two. And the more we played, the more Amanda understood that fifty-six means five groups of ten, plus six ones. The words meant something to her; they were no longer just a chant.

W hen Verity saw the number 34

she thought of thirty-four individual numbers:

GRADES

second and third

MATERIALS

**two sheets of paper
pencil
twenty paper cups
a large collection (at least 200) of
dried beans or paper clips for
counting
a deck of cards (Aces, Twos,
picture cards, and Jokers
removed)**

But she didn't appreciate a second meaning that underlies 34—namely, three groups of ten and four ones:

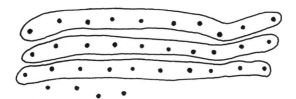

When a child understands this second meaning, he realizes that the 3 in 34 has a very different value than the 3 in 63 or 53; and that the 4 in 34 tells about the same amount as the 4 in 94 but a different amount than the 4 in 41. Most children find this a difficult concept to master, and Verity was no exception. Luckily, there are good games that help children meet this math challenge. COLLECT TEN is one of the best.

First Verity and I got our supplies together. We each drew a COLLECT TEN board on a blank sheet of paper:

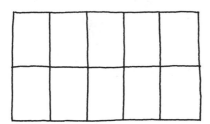

We filled a bowl with dried kidney beans. (You can substitute paper clips or any other small items. Just make sure you have at least two hundred of whatever you use.) Then we needed twenty paper cups: ten for Verity, ten for me. We also needed a shuffled deck of playing cards with Aces, Twos, pictures cards, and Jokers removed. Supplies in hand, we were ready to play.

The goal of the game is to collect one hundred beans. You collect ten beans per cup, then you collect ten cups—and you've got one hundred beans. Victory!

"Can I go first this time?" I asked.

"No," Verity declared. "I want to." Verity was an old hand at this game and knew that the person who went first had an advantage.

"Well, go ahead," I said.

She picked a card from the top of the deck. It was a Seven. She knew what that meant. She dipped her hand into the bowl and counted out exactly seven beans. Then she placed them carefully, one bean to a box, on her COLLECT TEN board.

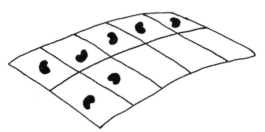

I picked up the next playing card. It was a Four. I took four beans from the bowl and set them on my board. "Looks like you're winning for the moment," I said.

"I know," she answered. "And it's my turn too." She picked an Eight and counted out eight beans from the bowl. "Hey," she said, looking at the beans in her hand, "I don't need all of these to fill up my board."

"Just use the beans you need to fill up the COLLECT TEN board and put the extras aside for a moment," I said. "Now take the ten beans on your board and pour them into a cup. That makes your first cup of ten. What's more, you have five beans left over. Put them on the board, and you're halfway to your second cup."

"When I get two cups, I'll have twenty. Then when I get ten cups full, I'll win the game," she said.

"Only if you get ten tens—otherwise known as one hundred—before me," I reminded her. "And now it's my turn." I took a card. "Oh, Verity, look what I got—a Ten!" I took ten beans from the bowl. "I don't even need to put these on my board. I can just take the whole set of ten and put it in a cup." I carefully counted ten beans and poured them directly into a cup without adding any beans at all to my playing board.

"There, now I have one cup of ten and four more. That's fourteen."

"Well, I have fifteen. That's better. If I get a ten this time, I'll have two cups full and five more—hey, that's twenty-five."

I was impressed with her display of mathematical thinking. I knew, too, that no amount of lecturing could have brought about this insight into numbers. Verity needed experience and concrete examples to make sense of these complex math ideas. How nice that she could get that experience while having such a good time.

The game advanced card by card, cup by cup, mathematical insight by mathematical insight, until, in about ten minutes time, Verity managed to collect one hundred beans and win the game.

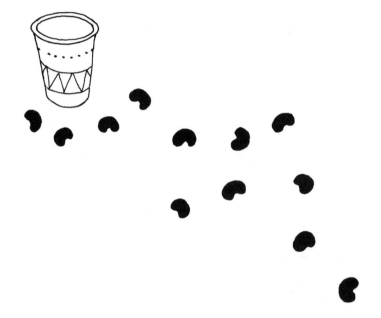

_T_his is a TARGET game board:

TARGET

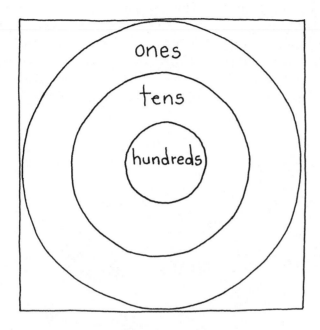

GRADES

second and third

MATERIALS

three sheets of paper
pencil
nine paper clips or pennies

You'll want to draw this board on a sheet of blank paper; a ruled sheet will make a very confusing target.

This is a TARGET scorecard:

You'll want two of these—one for you and one for your child.

Here's how to play. Throw nine paper clips onto the target. All the clips must land in one or another circle. If a clip misses a circle, pick it up and throw again, and if a clip lands on the line, give it a little shove to clarify its place. When all nine clips are properly located, you have to fill out the scorecard, beginning at the center. How many clips in the hundreds circle? How many in the tens circle? How many in the ones circle? Each figure goes neatly on the scorecard. If your TARGET board looks like this:

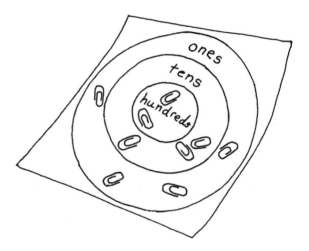

your scorecard will look like this:

If your TARGET board looks like this:

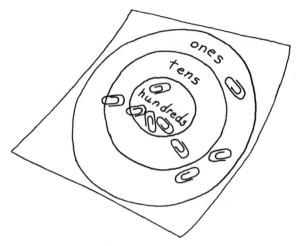

your scorecard will look like this:

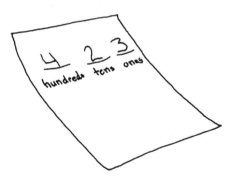

Your child takes the next turn. Whoever has the highest score wins the round. You can play as many rounds as you want—just draw more dashes on the score cards. I usually declare that five rounds make a game, though your child may insist on more.

This simple game is a good way to teach children that the placement of digits affects value. The numbers 234 and 423 each contain a 2, a 3, and a 4. Nevertheless, a score of 423 beats 234. That's how our number system works—a digit in the hundreds place is worth a lot more than the same digit in the ones place. If you understand the place value system, certain math calculations are a snap. For instance, it's as easy to add 1 to a number as it is to add 10 or 100. Start with 234. Add 1: you only change the ones place, and you get 235. Add 10: you only change the tens place, and you get 244. Add 100: you only change the hundreds place, and you get 334. How can your child better understand this wonderful system? A little TARGET practice will help.

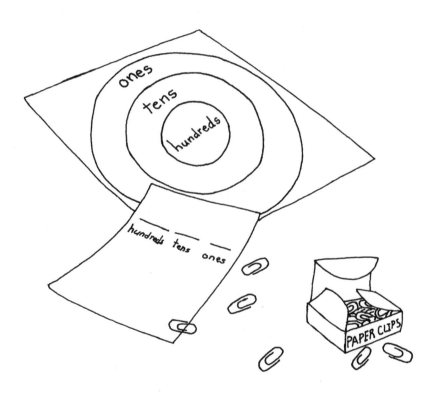

THE REARRANGE CONNECTION

Let's say you have thirty-five dollars—three ten-dollar bills and five singles—and you owe me eight dollars. How can you pay? You don't have enough one-dollar bills. So you go to the bank. You explain the problem to the teller. The teller says, "Fear not. Just give me one of your ten-dollar bills and I'll switch it for ten one-dollar bills. There. Now you have two ten-dollar bills and fifteen singles."

The teller didn't increase or decrease your money. He merely changed your three tens and five ones into two tens and fifteen ones. The total was the same, but with the money in this new form, you could handle the payment problem easily. This is exactly what happens when you "borrow" in subtraction. You rearrange numbers. To solve 42 minus 9, you rearrange 42. You call it three tens and twelve ones. Now you're ready to subtract.

Children can, of course, learn to compute 42 minus 9 using rote procedures. They learn to recite, in a singsong fashion: "Borrow from the four, you get three. Give to the two, you get twelve." Singsong knowledge is unreliable, however. Unless the child remembers every part of the chant and does everything in the right order, he'll make mistakes, get confused and frustrated, and will feel that math is not for him. It may take longer to teach the mathematical ideas behind "borrowing," but the effort pays off.

Most teachers nowadays appreciate how important it is for children to understand their math work and not just sing the chants. It's likely, therefore, that your child will already know a lot about rearranging numbers by third grade. The child will probably know more than you did at the same age. Still, a little help at home is always useful. Why not try THE REARRANGE CONNECTION?

It will take you about ten minutes to make the game board and cards, plus another ten minutes to play. If you like the game, store the board and cards in a drawer somewhere. Then you'll be set for future games of THE REARRANGE CONNECTION.

GRADE

third

MATERIALS

paper
pen
nine index cards cut into fourths
a collection of pennies and dimes
for game markers (any other
small objects will do)

Copy this game board onto a sheet of blank paper:

33	54	71	25	99	46
65	84	73	18	43	67
66	19	76	50	38	82
48	21	80	27	41	98
87	96	55	35	73	32
64	59	31	91	29	15

Now you need thirty-six game cards. Nine index cards cut into fourths will do. Here are thirty-six rearranged numbers for you to copy, one on each card:

2tens 13ones	4tens 14ones	6tens 11ones	1ten 15ones	8tens 19ones	3tens 16ones
5tens 15ones	7tens 14ones	6tens 13ones	0tens 18ones	3tens 13ones	5tens 17ones
5tens 16ones	0tens 19ones	6tens 16ones	4tens 10ones	2tens 18ones	7tens 12ones
3tens 18ones	1ten 11ones	7tens 10ones	1ten 17ones	3tens 11ones	8tens 18ones
7tens 17ones	8tens 16ones	4tens 15ones	2tens 15ones	6tens 13ones	2tens 12ones
5tens 14ones	4tens 19ones	2tens 11ones	8tens 11ones	1ten 19ones	0tens 15ones

Each number on the board is matched by a rearranged number on a card. 33 is on the board—2 tens 13 ones is on a card. 54 is on the board—4 tens 14 ones is on a card.

Now you need about eighteen pennies and eighteen dimes. If you don't have enough change, other small objects will do—dried beans or bits of cut-up paper, for instance. One set of markers is for you; the other set is for your child.

Shuffle the cards and place them face down on the table. Now, pick a card.

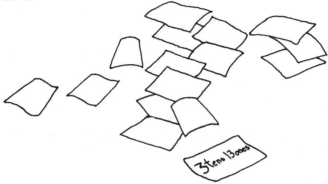

3 tens 13 ones

Study the rearranged number. Can you figure out the original number? Find it on the board and cover it with one of your game markers.

33	54	71	25	99	46
65	84	73	18	🏛	67
66	19	76	50	38	82
48	21	80	27	41	98
87	96	55	35	73	32
64	59	31	91	29	15

Now it's your child's turn. He picks a card, matches the rearranged number with the original on the playing board, and covers the spot with his marker.

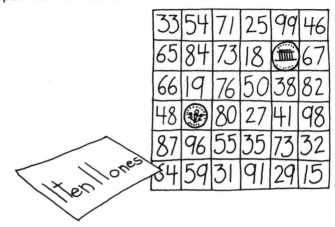

Continue taking turns until one player links up four markers. You can link markers in a straight line, like this:

or this:

or this:

You can also link markers in a bent line, like this:

or this:

The first player to connect four markers wins THE REARRANGE CONNECTION.

True, the game isn't as elegant as chess. Never mind: it does what it's supposed to do. It makes children think carefully about expressing the same amount in mathematically different ways. Surely Bobby Fischer himself didn't learn this particular lesson in any more pleasing way.

chapter 8

Addition and Subtraction

Addition and subtraction account for more than 50 percent of first-, second-, and third-grade math textbooks. Typically, therefore, your child spends half his math time during early school years learning, refining, and perfecting these two mathematical operations.

In the process, your child discovers that addition is the way you combine numbers and subtraction is how you take away or show the difference between numbers. Initially he'll count forward and backwards, usually aided by trustworthy fingers, to solve problems. He may find subtraction a lot harder than addition—many children do—but soon he'll get the knack of it. Over time, he'll memorize 232 basic addition and subtraction problems. He'll add and subtract to solve word problems. By the end of second grade, he'll handle problems with large numbers. He'll learn to "carry" numbers when adding and "borrow" when subtracting. He'll develop the ability to add and subtract larger numbers in his head without relying on paper and pencil. All that by the end of third grade!

Some of the work is pretty tedious, especially memorizing dozens of addition and subtraction facts. How to enliven the task? A card game called WAR will help. Learning to add and subtract large numbers isn't tedious, but it can prove difficult. A dice game called 500 SHAKEDOWN makes the effort fun. Your child will also need experience calculating in his mind without paper and pencil. When it's time for such calculations, a card game called SUITS UP, SUITS DOWN can add pleasure to the work.

In this chapter you'll find WAR, 500 SHAKEDOWN, SUITS UP, SUITS DOWN, and six other addition and subtraction games.

How will you know which games are right for your child? Look for the suggested grade levels at the beginning of each game. Although older children can always play games designed for

younger children and will usually benefit, the reverse is not true. Younger children do not benefit from playing games that are too hard. So pay attention to the grade levels, and after that, the choice is up to you. Does a game sound fun? Can you set aside a few minutes to play today or tomorrow? Then give it a try. If the game is a hit, don't be afraid to play it over and over. Your child will get valuable drill time, even if, to your mind, ninety-nine games of WAR seems more than enough.

IN AND OUT

A first-grade teacher called me about John, who was suffering terribly with math. John was a fluent reader, and a top-notch writer, but numbers baffled him completely. At math time he sank into misery, and escaped from misery by daydreaming. According to his teacher, John spent the greater part of every math period on a remote planet. His teacher felt one-to-one tutoring might bring him back to mathematical earth.

I gave a lot of thought to John's problem. Any math work that would succeed with him needed to pass three tests. First, the activity had to completely involve him. There could be no room for daydreaming. Second, the activity had to give him a rush of math success. He had to feel, from the start, that he could have shining moments in math just as he did in reading and writing. Third, the activity had to be fun. From past experience, I believed a game called IN AND OUT would do perfectly. Of course, trying the game with John was the only way to know for sure.

Here's how we played. I put a large salad bowl on the floor. Standing a couple of feet away, I tossed five paper clips, one clip at a time, at the bowl. The better my aim, the more clips in the bowl. After tossing the fifth clip, I counted: two clips in the bowl, three clips out. I recorded the results on a scorecard.

Then it was John's turn. He had to stand the same distance from the bowl and toss the same five paper clips. Would he get more in than me? If so, he'd win round one.

He did it! He got three clips in and two clips out.

We played five rounds in all. John won three rounds and I won two. John was the grand winner. What's more, in the fourth round, he tossed a perfect five in.

How had IN AND OUT fared in its three tests? First test: Did the game hold John's attention? Yes, not only during his tossing and recording, but during my tossing and recording as well. Test two: Did John have an important mathematical experience—an experience that left him feeling mathematically competent? Yes, as he threw the clips, John learned a lot about the number five. He learned that five could be three in and two out, or one in and four out, or two in and three out. Five is never three in and three out. Some combinations make five and others do not. By the time we finished the game, John was making comments like, "You only got one in. That means there are four out." Yet he hadn't counted. He hadn't used his fingers. Instead, he'd used newly gained knowledge about the number five. I complimented him on his astute mathematical reasoning and he burst into giggles. Test three: Did John have fun? He was beaming.

IN AND OUT passed the test with John. Perhaps it will in your house as well. By the way, you can change the number of clips anytime you want. You can toss four clips, six clips, eight clips, or any number up to about twelve. After which, playing gets too difficult and the paper clips start disappearing under the couch.

NUMBERBOW

GRADES

kindergarten and first

MATERIALS

two sheets of paper
pencil
crayons or colored pencils
dice

Sara loved beautiful colors. She loved dressing in bright purples, pinks, yellows, reds, and greens. Every time we worked together, I complimented her on her brilliant selections. Her fashion sense led to a colorful new addition game.

I made two identical boards that looked like this:

I showed them to her.

"Oh," she said. "These look like rainbows."

"They are, in a way. We're even going to use crayons to color the different boxes. Only you can't color just any box. You have to throw two dice, add up the numbers, and whatever answer you get, you color. If you already colored that number, you're stuck until your next turn. We both take ten turns. After that we compare and see who has the most colorful rainbow. The one with the most colors is the winner."

"Can I use any colors I want?" Sara asked.

"Any colors in my crayon collection. It's your rainbow," I replied.

"It's really a NUMBERBOW," she said with a laugh.

"You're right. That's a great name for this game. From now on it's called NUMBERBOW."

We began the game. Sara tossed the dice and came up with a three and a four. She wasn't sure how to add these numbers. I suggested she count the dots on the dice. She did and got her total: seven. Sara chose a red crayon and began coloring her NUMBERBOW.

Then it was my turn. I tossed double twos. My score? Four. I selected purple for my first color.

Sara took a second turn. She rolled a two and a five. Seven again. Her seven was already bright red. There was nothing to do but pass the dice back to me. We kept playing until we'd each had ten turns. In the end, my NUMBERBOW was more colorful. Sara wasn't discouraged, however. In fact, she wanted to play again— right away. And so we did. We played twice more that day and many more times in the weeks that followed. NUMBERBOW became a regular feature of Sara's tutoring time. Initially she counted dots on the dice or used her fingers to get her score. Then some of the combinations became automatic. By the time Sara was bored with NUMBERBOW, she'd memorized all the possible addition combinations you can make with two dice.

During our first games, Sara and I got so carried away we forgot to keep track of our turns.

"Was that your sixth or seventh throw?" I'd ask.

"I don't remember," Sara answered.

We came up with a solution to this problem. We kept track of our turns with tally marks. Every time we took a turn, we drew a small slash on the bottom of our game boards. That way, we always knew how many turns we'd used up and how many chances remained to color our NUMBERBOWS.

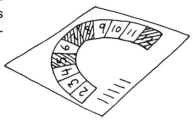

NUMBER CHAIN

NUMBER CHAIN is a completely portable ten-minute game. You can play anywhere you have a piece of paper and a pencil. It's a good train game. It's not a bad car game either (as long as you're not driving). Or you might want to play it while you're waiting for cookies to come out of the oven.

The first time I played with Matthew, I knew it was a hit. I explained the rules:

"We're going to make a NUMBER CHAIN. A NUMBER CHAIN is made up of addition and subtraction problems. First I give you a problem to answer, then you give me one. I win if I catch you making an addition or subtraction mistake. You win if you catch me making a mistake. Here's the tricky part. I promise that some time during the game I *will* make a mistake. I'll make a mistake that's hard to catch, but if you find it, you win. Here's one more important rule. All the problems must link together like a chain. You'll see how that works as we play."

I wrote down the first problem.

$$3 + 5$$

Matthew took up a pencil and supplied the answer.

$$3 + 5 = 8$$

"Great," I said. "Now give me a problem. You can't make it any old problem, however. The problem must begin with eight. It could be an addition problem: eight plus three, or eight plus two, or eight plus ten. It could be a subtraction problem: eight minus two, or eight minus five. Tell me the problem you want and I'll show you how to put it on the chain."

Matthew thought a bit. Then he announced, "I want eight plus six."

"That's a good choice. Here's how to write it:

$$3 + 5 = 8 \quad 8 + 6 =$$

Now I'll fill in the answer and give you a new problem."

$$3+5=8 \quad 8+6=14 \quad 14-4=$$

As soon as he saw 14 − 4, Matthew started to subtract. I interrupted him. "Wait a minute. You better check my answer first. What if I made a mistake? You wouldn't want to miss it and lose a chance to win the game."

Matthew began adding. When he'd determined that eight and six did make fourteen, he turned his attention to 14 − 4.

$$3+5=8 \quad 8+6=14 \quad 14-4=10$$

Finally, he added to the chain:

$$3+5=8 \quad 8+6=14 \quad 14-4=10 \quad 10+100000$$

"Wow!" I exclaimed. "That's a big addition problem. But Matthew, what if I make my mistake now? Will you know if the answer is wrong? You have to know the answer yourself before you can correct me."

Matthew groaned. I told him he could substitute a different number for one hundred thousand. He quickly erased almost all the zeros, leaving behind a more sensible problem.

$$3+5=8 \quad 8+6=14 \quad 14-4=10 \quad 10+10=$$

My turn.

$$3+5=8 \quad 8+6=14 \quad 14-4=10 \quad 10+10=22 \quad 22-1=$$

Matthew was so intent on solving 22 − 1, he forgot to check my arithmetic. He picked up his pencil and started right in

After he'd written:

$$3+5=8 \quad 8+6=14 \quad 14-4=10 \quad 10+10=22 \quad 22-1=21$$

I lowered the boom, lightly.

"I tricked you, Matthew. Ten plus ten doesn't equal twenty-two. You missed my mistake. You'll have to catch me in another one if you want to win the game." Even though I had to correct Matthew, I tried not to sound judgmental. After all, Matthew felt bad enough about his lost opportunity.

The game continued. Matthew added a problem to the chain and I answered it:

$$3+5=8 \quad 8+6=14 \quad 14-4=10 \quad 10+10=22 \quad 22-1=21 \quad 21-3=12$$

"That's not right," Matthew shouted. "That's not right. Twenty-one take away three isn't twelve. You broke the chain. I caught you!"

Winning certainly makes a child happy.

I used simple math problems for Matthew's chain. Matthew wasn't ready for harder stuff. With older children and math whizzes, weightier chains are in order. Here are a few links from a chain game played with Elizabeth:

$$145+314=459 \quad 459-267=192 \quad 192+648=840$$

Did Elizabeth and I calculate these problems in our heads? No. We did do some work in our heads, but for the rest, a little scrap paper came in handy.

Here's an ADDITION/SUBTRAC-
TION TIC-TAC-TOE board:

7-3	8+7	2+1
8-5	6+4	6-4
10-3	3+7	8+3

It's identical to a regular board, except nine unsolved addition and subtraction problems appear in the grid. You play ADDITION/ SUBTRACTION TIC-TAC-TOE just like the regular game, with one exception. Before placing an X or O in your chosen spot, you must solve the math problem. In the five minutes you spend playing the game, therefore, your child will solve four or five problems.

What problems should you put on the board? You can include any you want. Even killers like 324 − 296 are okay, if your child can handle them. For younger children, however, ADDITION/SUB-TRACTION TIC-TAC-TOE should stay pretty simple. Below you'll find a list of 232 problems that youngsters are expected to commit to memory before the end of third grade, and you should probably stick to these problems.

The list includes problems at three levels of difficulty: easy, toughies, and super-toughies. The best thing is to start picking from among the easy problems. Then gradually mix in a few tough-ies, and later on a few more. Later still, a few super-toughies. But there should always be some easy problems. Easy problems give a child a chance to review, keep his confidence, and make ADDITION/SUBTRACTION TIC-TAC-TOE challenging but not backbreaking.

It may not be immediately apparent why one problem is easy, another a toughie, and a third a super-toughie, but take my word for it.

121 Addition Problems

Easy

0+0	0+1	0+2	0+3	0+4	0+5	0+6
0+7	0+8	0+9	0+10	1+0	2+0	3+0
4+0	5+0	6+0	7+0	8+0	9+0	10+0
1+1	1+2	1+3	1+4	1+5	1+6	1+7
1+8	1+9	1+10	2+1	2+2	2+3	2+4
2+5	2+6	2+7	2+8	2+9	2+10	3+1
3+2	3+3	3+4	4+1	4+2	4+3	4+4
5+1	5+2	5+3	5+5	6+1	6+2	6+3
7+1	7+2	7+3	8+1	8+2	9+1	9+2
10+1	10+2	10+3	10+4	10+10		

Toughies

3+5	3+6	3+7	3+8	3+9	3+10	4+5
4+6	4+7	4+8	4+9	4+10	5+4	5+6
8+5	8+10	9+3	9+4	9+5	9+10	10+5
10+6	10+7	10+8	10+9			

Super-toughies

5+7	5+8	5+9	5+10	6+4	6+5	6+6
6+7	6+8	6+9	6+10	7+4	7+5	7+6
7+7	7+8	7+9	7+10	8+3	8+4	8+6
8+7	8+8	8+9	9+6	9+7	9+8	9+9

111 Subtraction Problems

Easy

0 − 0	1 − 0	2 − 0	3 − 0	4 − 0	5 − 0	6 − 0
7 − 0	8 − 0	9 − 0	10 − 0	1 − 1	2 − 1	3 − 1
4 − 1	5 − 1	6 − 1	7 − 1	8 − 1	9 − 1	10 − 1
2 − 2	3 − 2	4 − 2	5 − 2	6 − 2	7 − 2	8 − 2
9 − 2	10 − 2	11 − 2	3 − 3	4 − 3	5 − 3	6 − 3
4 − 4	5 − 4	6 − 4	5 − 5	6 − 5	7 − 5	6 − 6
7 − 6	8 − 6	7 − 7	8 − 7	9 − 7	8 − 8	9 − 8
9 − 9	10 − 9	10 − 10				

Toughies

7 − 3	8 − 3	9 − 3	10 − 3	11 − 3	12 − 3	7 − 4
8 − 4	9 − 4	10 − 4	11 − 4	12 − 4	13 − 4	8 − 5
9 − 5	10 − 5	11 − 5	9 − 6	10 − 6	11 − 6	12 − 6
10 − 7	11 − 7	10 − 8	11 − 8	11 − 9	11 − 10	12 − 10
13 − 10	14 − 10	15 − 10	16 − 10	17 − 10	18 − 10	19 − 10

Super-toughies

12 − 5	13 − 5	14 − 5	13 − 6	14 − 6	15 − 6	12 − 7
13 − 7	14 − 7	15 − 7	16 − 7	12 − 8	13 − 8	14 − 8
15 − 8	16 − 8	17 − 8	12 − 9	13 − 9	14 − 9	15 − 9
16 − 9	17 − 9	18 − 9				

WAR

GRADES

first, second, and third

MATERIALS

a deck of cards (picture cards
and Jokers removed)

WAR is hell. No one in their right mind wants a WAR—unless it's the playing-card version. Then everyone wants in on the action.

You probably already know the card game. You and your child evenly split a deck of cards. Each of you turns over the top card in your card arsenal. You compare numbers. Whoever has the highest number captures both cards. If the numbers are identical you declare a war. The battle involves slapping three cards face down while saying loudly, "I—de—clare—war." On the word "war," you turn a fourth card face up. The player with the highest number showing wins all the battle cards! If the two cards are again the same (a rare event), you have a double war. The game goes on and on until one player captures the entire deck. This takes time. It's not easy winning a war.

Most children like WAR so much they even like the game in its addition and subtraction versions. To play addition WAR, you must remove all picture cards and Jokers from the deck. Then divide the remaining cards as usual. But instead of turning over one card at a time, turn over two cards and add the numbers. The combatant with the highest sum wins all four cards.

If the sums are the same, WAR must be declared. WAR means that three cards are slapped face down while saying "I declare . . ." and two cards are shot face up on the word "war." Each player adds the numbers on his upturned cards, and the highest total wins.

Danny hated practicing addition facts. Worksheets made him anxious. Flash cards made him jittery. But Danny loved playing WAR. After a few rounds, he blurted out, "I know I'm learning, but it's so much fun it doesn't feel like learning."

From our first skirmishes, however, I noticed that Danny was using math skills other than addition to determine the winner. Once, I had a Five and an Eight turned over and Danny had a Five and a Ten.

"I win," he announced the moment he saw the cards.

"How do you know?" I asked.

"You have five and I have five. That's the same. But I have ten and you only have eight, so I win."

Impeccable logic, terrific math thinking. I wanted to encourage this kind of thought, so I praised him mightily for his judgment. I wanted him to continue adding, however. To this end, I made a rule of WAR. Danny could use his brilliant mathematical analysis to proclaim the winner, but he still had to add up his cards and announce the results. He agreed to my terms, as long as I did the same.

Danny would have happily played WAR hour after hour. I preferred calling a truce after about ten minutes—we had other, less bloody, work to attend to, after all. WAR usually take longer than ten minutes to finish, however. Here's how we solved this problem. We played for ten minutes. Then we wrapped and labeled our cards.

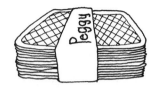

We stashed the cards on a shelf, ready and waiting until the next round of hostilities.

You can do the same at your house. Start a game of WAR and play for ten minutes before preparing dinner, before watching TV, or before bath time. When ten minutes are up and the food is hot, the show is on, or the tub is full, put the cards away until next time. Perhaps, though, your child isn't one for waiting to find out the winner. In that case, when the ten minutes of WAR are over, count your cards. The player with the largest stack is the winner.

If WAR creates a sensation at your house, you can also try a subtraction variation. Instead of adding, subtract the smaller from the larger number on your two cards. The warrior with the smaller answer wins the round—and the cards.

Sophie found math boring. Nothing about 7 + 9 had any intrinsic interest for her. I found it easy, however, to rivet her attention by tucking addition and subtraction problems neatly inside NUMBER STORIES.

In a faraway land lived a brave princess. The princess wanted to save her country from a terrible dragon. The dragon had crushed seven barns and set fire to nine houses. *(How many buildings did the dragon destroy?)* The dragon's power came from his eleven magic teeth. To save her country, the princess had to remove at least four magic dragon teeth. Then the dragon wouldn't have enough magic to do any harm. *(How many teeth would he have then?)*

The princess had a plan. She ordered her royal candy makers to prepare the gooiest, sweetest candies ever made. Then she took a nine-pound bag in her left hand, a nine-pound bag in her right hand (*How many pounds altogether?*), and set off to find the dragon. He was lurking in a cave. The princess offered the dragon some candy. He was delighted. The princess fed him and fed him the candy treats. The dragon ate five pounds immediately. Then he ate six more pounds. Then he ate another four pounds. *(How much did he eat?)* Soon the dragon complained of a toothache.

The princess said, "Don't worry, I'm a dentist." She climbed into the dragon's mouth and started pulling teeth. The dragon was groaning, so he didn't notice. The princess pulled six of the dragon's eleven teeth. *(How many teeth did the dragon have now?)* The dragon lost his magic power! He agreed to live peacefully in the princess's castle. Every day he ate seven pounds of candy in the morning and five pounds in the evening *(How much more did he eat in the morning?)* and never did another evil deed. He had no time. Chewing candy took every moment from morning to night.

A dragon, a brave princess, and gooey candies made math vivid and exciting for Sophie. When it meant finding out how many buildings were decimated by an evil dragon, solving 7 + 9 became important and interesting. That's why I made a point of beginning all of Sophie's tutoring sessions with a story. These stories weren't especially artistic or profound. I freely stole ideas from fairy tales and movie plots.

For Sophie, I used numbers that are relatively easy to add and subtract, but you can make the math more challenging for older, more experienced mathematicians. If your child has difficulty figuring out the math problem, help all you can. Draw a picture. Rephrase the math question to make it easier to understand. Change from larger numbers to smaller numbers. Remember, your child wants to show off his addition and subtraction powers. It makes him feel good about math and about himself. If the problems are too hard, the story will bog down, and the whole exercise will be a pointless bore. So keep the problems simple.

Here are two stories to get you going.

Bella Bunny needed carrots. She wanted to make a special treat for her children. Bella had six girl bunnies and three boy bunnies. *(How many children does Bella have?)* She gathered four carrots from Mr. Brown's garden and five carrots from Ms. Green's garden. *(How many carrots did she have in all?)* Bella wanted to make a carrot cake. To make the cake, she needed twelve carrots. *(How many more carrots does she need?)* There was only one more garden to try, Jeremy Giant's. Bella was afraid to go to Jeremy's garden, but she had no choice. She took three little hops, six middle-sized hops, and seven jumbo hops to get to the gate. *(How many hops did Bella hop?)* Bella slipped under the gate. She saw seven carrots in a wheelbarrow. "I will just take three of them," she said to herself. *(How many carrots will be*

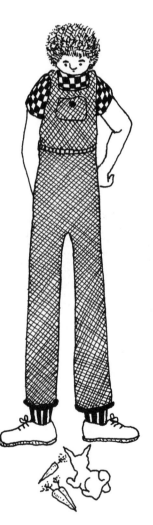

left in the wheelbarrow?) She started to take the carrots, when an enormous hand fell on her head. "What are you doing in my garden?" said Jeremy Giant in a gruff voice. "Oh, please don't hurt me," said Bella. "I need these carrots to make a carrot cake for my little bunnies."

"Carrot cake," said the giant. "I love carrot cake. I will let you go if you promise to make me ten carrot cakes."

Bella promised, but she needed more carrots. Jeremy gave her all she wanted. Bella made the giant seven cakes on Monday. *(How many more cakes does she need to make?)* On Tuesday she made the rest of the cakes. This made Jeremy so happy that he let Bella come into his garden any time at all and take all the carrots she wanted—just so long as she made him some yummy cakes to eat.

Paul wanted to be a magician. All day long he practiced tricks. He practiced three hours every morning and three hours every afternoon. *(How many hours did he practice each day?)* He practiced seven card tricks and five disappearing tricks. *(How many more card tricks did he practice?)* Still, he couldn't get a single trick to work. This made him sad. "I need help," Paul said. He went to the bookstore to buy some magic books. He found a book that cost five dollars and another book that cost eight dollars. Paul bought them both. *(How much money did he spend?)* Paul read the first magic book, but it didn't help. He started the second book. It was really strange. On the first page it said, "Boil this book in water for sixteen minutes, then dry it for exactly seven minutes." *(How many minutes of work in all?)* "Sleep with the book under your pillow. The book must be open for four hours and closed for four hours." *(How many hours is that?)* Paul followed the instructions. When he woke up the

next morning, he felt thirsty. "I wish I had a glass of juice," he said. Suddenly a glass of juice appeared in his hand. Paul was amazed. He made four more wishes. They all came true. He made ten more wishes. They all came true. He made three more wishes. They came true too. *(How many wishes did he make?)* Paul knew the truth. His book was *really* a magic book! Paul read more of the book. He discovered that if he slept on the book every night, he would get exactly twenty wishes the next day. *(How many more wishes does Paul have for today?)* Paul was delighted. He figured out how many wishes he'd have in two days *(How many?)*, in three days *(How many?)*, and in four days *(How many?)*, before sitting down to breakfast. From that day on, Paul was the most famous magician on earth. No one knew how he did his tricks, and Paul never gave away the secret.

Perhaps someday soon your child will want to make up NUMBER STORIES filled with problems for you to solve. And then . . . oh, the tales you'll hear.

SUITS UP, SUITS DOWN is a game that helps children calculate sums in their heads. There are several versions, each one harder than the last. The easiest version requires ten cards, the Ace through Ten of a single suit (the Ace, of course, has a value of one).

GRADES

second and third

MATERIALS

a deck of cards (picture cards and Jokers removed)

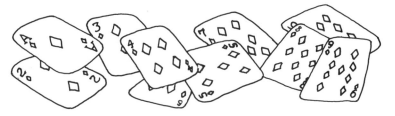

Shuffle the cards and stack them face down. Now turn over the top card.

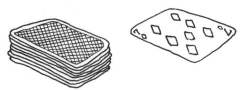

Seven. That's your starting number. Turn over another card.

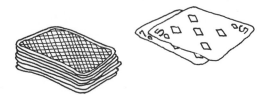

Five. Add five to seven and you get twelve. Turn over a third card.

Three. Add three to twelve and you get fifteen.

Add the fourth card, then the fifth. By now you may be tempted to use a paper and pencil to determine your sum, but that's not allowed. In this game, everything has to be done in your head. So keep turning over cards and making mental calculations. When you add the tenth card, you should have exactly fifty-five. Is your total something else? You slipped up. But don't worry, you can always take another turn. In fact, you can take another turn even if you correctly hit fifty-five. Reshuffle the ten cards. You'll get a new numerical arrangement, and, therefore, a new set of addition problems.

Here's a second version of SUITS UP, SUITS DOWN. Use the same ten cards. This time, though, start with the number fifty-five and subtract as you turn over cards. When you subtract the tenth card, you should hit zero.

Want a version that's twice as hard? Use two suits, making twenty cards altogether. Now you should add up to 110, or subtract from 110 down to zero. How about three suits? With thirty cards you get up to 165. Finally, put all four suits into play. Now you must mentally calculate up to or down from 220!

I played this game with Ben, a young math whiz. Ben took great pride in his remarkable ability to calculate without paper and pencil. This game offered him the perfect opportunity to show his stuff, and he loved it. But would a less advanced student enjoy the game too? I tried it with Renée, a third-grader who struggles with math. The game wasn't easy for Renée. Nevertheless, the first time we played, with a hint or two from me, she did fifty-five. A great accomplishment!

Renée and I played SUITS UP, SUITS DOWN many times in the coming months. It was a perfect five-minute warm-up for our tutoring sessions. I was careful not to overtax her. I let her play the simplest version—adding with a single suit—for many weeks before even suggesting something different. Eventually I proposed two-suit addition. She liked the change. Renée was pleased with how well she handled so many cards. In time, I introduced her to the subtraction version of SUITS UP, SUITS DOWN. Like many children, Renée found subtraction harder and more frustrating than addition. For Renée, adding twenty cards up to 110 was, in fact, easier than subtracting ten cards from fifty-five down to zero. Soon, however, Renée could subtract with a calculator's precision.

Give SUITS UP, SUITS DOWN a try. In less than ten minutes you'll know if it gets thumbs-up or thumbs-down in your house.

BOXED
NUMBERS

MATERIALS

paper
pencil
a deck of cards (Tens, picture
cards, and Jokers removed)

"**A**ll right, Josh, get to work," I said. "Here's a deck of cards. We have to remove the picture cards, Jokers, and Tens, and then shuffle the deck. Can you do that?"

"Sure," Josh said.

"Good. I'll get our game pages ready." I took two sheets of paper and drew boxes.

 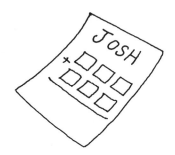

"Hey, that looks like an addition problem," said Josh when he saw his page.

"You're right. It's an addition problem without numbers," I said. I went on to explain the game rules. I told Josh that we were going to fill our boxes with numbers and then add. The winner in this game is the player with the biggest total. How would we select numbers to put in the boxes? We'd pick playing cards. Card by card, digit by digit, we'd fill the top number from the right to left and then the bottom number from right to left.

I showed Josh how this worked by picking cards and writing numbers. The first card I selected was an Eight. I filled in my first box.

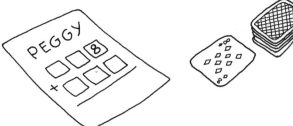

Then I got Six. I filled in a box.

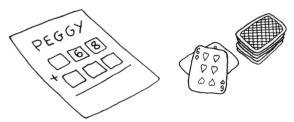

Unfortunately, my next card was a Three. Getting a lowly three in the hundreds place was poor pickings indeed.

I was ready to fill in the bottom number. I picked an Ace. Ace equals one.

Next I got a Four.

Four wasn't the best number in the deck, but at least I'd avoided another ace.

My last number was a Three.

I was ready to add.

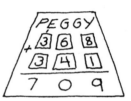

My grand total was 709. "Well, Josh," I said. "I had pretty good luck. You'll have a hard time topping that."

Josh picked his cards, moaning when he got low numbers and delighted with the high ones.

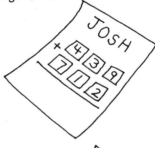

He added.

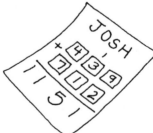

And he won.

While Josh was feeling the flush of victory, I challenged him to a second round. Now, however, I set up the boxes differently.

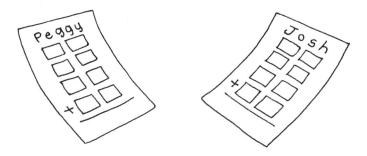

The same game rules applied. The third time we played, the boxes looked like this:

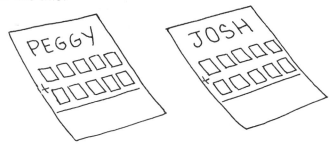

A week later, we played subtraction BOXED NUMBERS. The main difference between the addition and subtraction versions rests in how you set up the boxes. In subtraction BOXED NUMBERS, you always play with at least one more box in the top row than in the bottom. That way you avoid the possibility of subtracting yourself into the realm of negative numbers, which is a scary place even for adults. Here are a few subtraction designs:

After many weeks of playing both addition and subtraction BOXED NUMBERS, Josh had a lovely insight into numbers. He looked at his page,

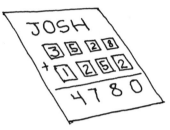

and then at my numbers, before I had a chance to add.

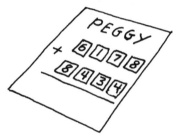

"You're going to win," he said. "You're adding two big numbers, and I added two small numbers." For the first time, Josh was thinking about numbers before he began to add. He was using mathematical intelligence to predict the winner without actually doing the arithmetic work. About a week later, he had a similar insight into subtraction. He looked at his game page,

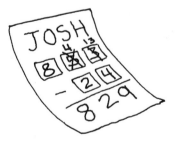

and then at mine, before I had a chance to subtract.

"I won," he said.

"How do you know?" I asked.

"Well, you've got a smaller number on the top than me, and you're taking away a bigger number, so you'll end up with less than me!"

I was thrilled listening to Josh's intelligent observations about subtraction. Just a few short weeks ago, he couldn't have employed this kind of logic. What happened to change his thinking? Experience. BOXED NUMBERS gave him so much experience with numbers—experience with winning and losing number combinations—that, on occasion, he could predict the winner without doing a calculation.

It got to the point where two-number BOXED NUMBERS had little to offer him, since he could immediately predict who won, except in close calls. Fortunately, Josh still couldn't tell if

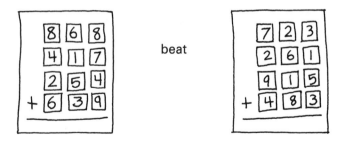

beat

without actually adding. So we stuck to multinumber, multidigit addition games and forgot about playing subtraction BOXED NUMBERS. That's how we kept the game suspenseful, appealing, and educational, even after Josh had developed number savvy.

500
SHAKEDOWN

GRADE

third

MATERIALS

paper
pencil
two dice

In 500 SHAKEDOWN, you and your child each start with 500 points. You take turns throwing a pair of dice. With the numbers on the dice, you make the biggest two-digit number you can. If you throw

the biggest two-digit number you can make is 42. Now you subtract this number from your initial 500 points.

$$\begin{array}{r} 500 \\ -42 \\ \hline 458 \end{array}$$

You keep tossing dice, making numbers, and subtracting—until one player can subtract only by going below zero. At which moment, that player wins.

There's one complication. When you throw a 1, the rules change. You don't subtract. Instead, you make the smallest two-digit number you can and *add*. If you throw

the smallest two-digit number is 15. So you take 15 and add it to your total.

$$\begin{array}{r} 458 \\ +15 \\ \hline 473 \end{array}$$

This rule keeps the score bouncing up and down.

Want a greater challenge? Start with 5,000 points and roll three dice. Greater yet? Start with 50,000 and role four dice. 500 SHAKE-DOWN can get pretty difficult, if you want it to. The game, needless to say, makes for a lot of practice in subtraction, and a little practice in addition. Plus, it has the excitement of a horse race.

chapter 9

Size and Shape

Pythagoras, ancient Greece's Father of Mathematics, believed that everything in the world is arranged according to measure, number, and mathematical shape. He created the Western musical scale by measuring strings on an instrument to follow set mathematical proportions. He defined the Golden Rectangle, a precisely measured and proportioned shape that forms the basis for classical architecture, sculpture, and painting. He developed his famous theorem about measuring the hypotenuse of any right-angle triangle, which is the basic element for all mechanics and technology. And how did he achieve these wonders? According to my theorem, his mom and dad must have played geometry and measurement games with him.

Geometry education begins when a youngster starts identifying basic shapes: circles, squares, triangles, and rectangles. This seems a simple task, but there are pitfalls for young children. Many a kindergartener and first-grader will automatically recognize this shape △ as a triangle but not know what to call these shapes:

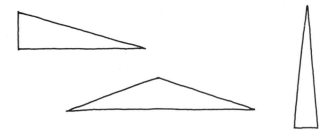

If your child draws triangles, plays with circles, and builds three-dimensional cubes, his understanding of geometric forms will deepen. He'll begin to instinctively understand the rules that govern the physical world. That's the goal of the first three games in this chapter. The next three games are measurement games. AN ODD MEASURE gets your child measuring in unusual ways. Play HOW LONG? and your child will learn about inches and centimeters. Maybe, though, your child would prefer spending ten minutes cooking some delicious goodies—TEN-MINUTE RECIPES—while, incidentally, learning to measure metric capacity. These are all useful games, and perhaps, who knows, by playing them, you may be nurturing your own Pythagoras.

FOLLOW THE SHAPE LEADER

When you play follow the leader, you walk, skip, hop, and tiptoe a twisty, swervy path, and your child tries to follow you. When you play FOLLOW THE SHAPE LEADER, your path doesn't twist or swerve. Instead, you deliberately outline geometric shapes by walking them: circles, squares, rectangles, triangles. And while walking each shape, announce what it is: "A circle—follow me!"

Beaches are the best place to play. Your feet drag through the sand, and the geometric shape emerges behind you. But any place at all will do, so long as you aren't knocking over the furniture.

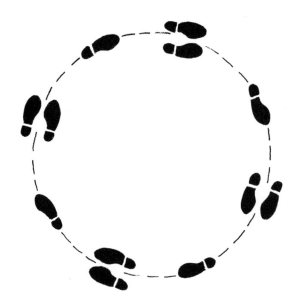

*C*ut off one of the points of a triangle, and you create a quadrilateral.

Cut certain triangles just right, and you get an especially pleasing quadrilateral called a trapezoid.

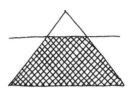

Put two triangles of the same size together in the correct way, and you can create one big triangle, or else a diamond, or else a rectangle.

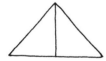 

If the triangles are equilateral, you can get a square.

Discoveries like these help initiate children into the world of geometry. My student James stumbled on these discoveries while making a SHAPELY DRAWING. He liked the game. It fitted his temperament, which was artistic.

SHAPELY DRAWING

GRADES

kindergarten, first, and second

MATERIALS

paper
pencil
cardboard, poster board, or
oaktag
crayons
scissors

Before we started, I cut a triangle from a piece of cardboard. I handed James the cutout, as well as a sheet of blank paper and a pencil, and I told him to trace the triangle on the paper as many times as he wanted. He could place the triangles anywhere he liked. He could overlap triangles. He could attach them. He could separate them. The choice was his.

James got to work. Sometimes he had difficulty holding the cutout still and needed my helping hand. Mostly, though, he drew triangle after triangle all on his own. After about five minutes, his paper was filled with triangles and the shapes triangles make when they overlap.

I didn't lecture James on the shapes he created. I did, however, enthusiastically greet various quadrilaterals and polygons as they emerged. To help James see these shapes more clearly, and to make the picture more beautiful, I gave him a box of crayons and suggested he color the shapes within the shapes. I offered to help with the coloring. Together, we made a lovely picture.

James's premiere SHAPELY DRAWING was a great success, combining art and geometry most gracefully. So I suggested a second drawing. This time, instead of a triangle, I gave James a cutout cardboard square, and he went to work tracing the square onto a blank page, creating new shapes by combining squares and coloring the shapes any way he felt.

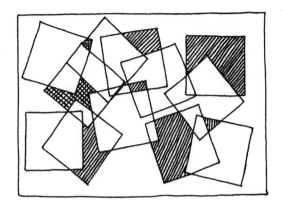

It was another masterpiece.
Over the weeks that followed, James worked with:

rectangles   trapezoids   hexagons

ovals   octagons   parallelograms   circles

rhombuses   pentagons   irregular quadrilaterals

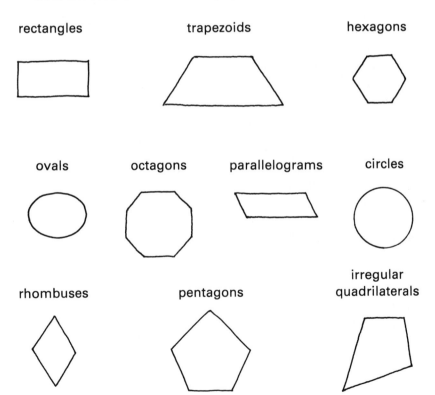

Sometimes I gave him several different cutouts to use in a single drawing. These pictures were particularly intricate and interesting.

I always used the correct geometric vocabulary to describe shapes. I didn't expect James to memorize the words, but I did want him to be familiar with the strange-sounding Greek terms.

One difficult aspect to geometry is the way shapes are categorized. All squares are rectangles, but not all rectangles are squares. All squares and rectangles are quadrilaterals, but not all quadrilaterals are squares or rectangles. The terms I used reflected these arrangements. Once I handed James a shape that looked like this:

and said, "Here's a rectangle."

"It's a square!" he said.

I answered, "You're right, it is a square. But I'm right too, because squares are special rectangles. Squares are rectangles where all the sides are the same length."

James didn't always understand my definitions, but they started him thinking. Geometry, he discovered, is more than meets the eye.

James was in second grade and could bear up under the confusing terms. With younger children, I keep the geometric vocabulary correct, but at a minimum. Too many words overwhelm young children. Too many words may overwhelm you, the adult, as well. In that case, don't worry about more than the simple words: square, circle, triangle, rectangle. The rest of the shapes can go unnamed. The key thing is to get the child to play with shapes and learn something about the nature of each geometric form that he draws!

The miracle of turning a flat piece of paper or oaktag into an amazing three-dimensional shape is not so difficult that you can't perform it, with the right coaching. Here, for instance, is how to make a box. Cut out a T-shaped piece of paper or oaktag. The T should be made up of six equal-sized squares defined by dotted lines, like this:

GRADES

second and third

MATERIALS

paper, poster board, or oaktag
pencil
scissors
ruler
transparent tape

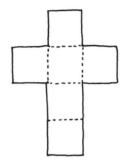

Fold along the dotted lines, tape them in place, and presto! A box.

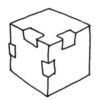

Did your child enjoy constructing the box? If so, other 3-D SHAPES may recommend themselves. The instructions below show how to make four shapes: a long box, a tent, a pyramid, and a diamond.

You can, of course, use correct geometrical names for these shapes. A box is called a cube, a long box is a square prism, a tent is a triangular prism, a pyramid is a square pyramid, a diamond is an octahedron. With young children, I tend not to employ geometric terminology for three-dimensional shapes. The names are bulky and difficult, unlike the more familiar two-dimensional words for designs.

Now, on to the long box.

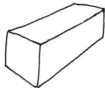

You build this box the same way as the square box, except that your starting shape will have the form of a pudgy T. The four main sections are equal-sized rectangles, while the sides are squares.

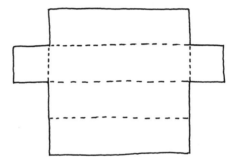

Fold along the dotted lines, tape the sizes together, and the long box will be yours.

A tent looks like this:

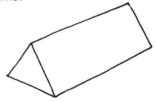

A sturdy tent is easy enough to construct. Start your work by cutting out a novel-looking shape made up of three rectangles and two equilateral triangles (triangles whose three sides are all the same size):

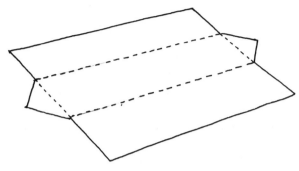

Fold, tape, and the tent is made.

Here's a pyramid:

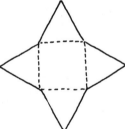

To create it, start with a square bordered by four equilateral triangles:

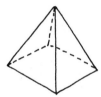

Fold along the dotted lines, and tape the sides. Pharaoh couldn't do better!

This is a diamond:

It's a little more complicated than the other shapes, but worth the extra effort. Begin with this collection of eight triangles.

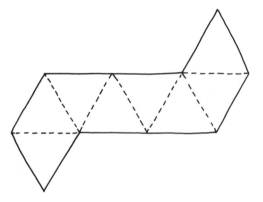

Start folding and you'll see the shape emerge. Tape the sides in place, and the diamond sparkles.

Over a few months, your child can build up quite a collection of 3-D SHAPES. He can use them for decoration (put a string through the shapes and dangle them from window latches or a Christmas tree). He can employ the shapes as building blocks, or smash them up. There's nothing wrong with getting up now and then to stomp a paper construction to the floor. Whatever happens to the 3-D SHAPES in the end, your child will have a chance to learn about geometric forms not only with his intellect but with his fingers.

How many pennies long is your index finger?

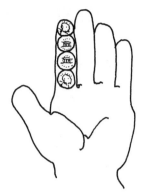

AN ODD MEASURE

GRADES

first and second

MATERIALS

various small objects (paper clips, pennies, dried beans, etc.)

How many kidney beans long is your pencil?

How many paper clips long is your hand?

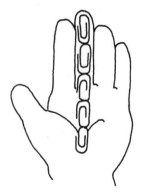

How many steps does it take your child to cross the living room? How many steps does it take you?

How does measuring in these strange ways help your child? Before children learn about standard measurement systems—centimeters and inches—they have to understand that you can measure the length and breadth of anything using any object. You can measure in pennies, paper clips, kidney beans, toothpicks, rubber bands, footsteps. My wristwatch, from one end of the band to the other, is 12 pennies long. It is also 6 AAA batteries long, or 5 iron nails long, or 4 jumbo paper clips long, or 7 small paper clips long, or 22 centimeters long, or 8½ inches long.

In ancient times, people used the human body to measure length: girth was the length around the waist; a cubit was the measure from elbow to the tip of the middle finger; a palm was the width of the hand; a span went from the tip of the thumb to the tip of the little finger; an ell was from the tip of the middle finger on an outstretched arm to the middle of the body; a fathom was from the tip of the middle finger to the tip of the other middle finger when both arms are stretched out. A mile was the distance a Roman army could travel in one hour. Measurements like these had advantages. The fabric dealer at the medieval fair never had to hunt for a ruler. On the other hand, not all girths, or ells, or spans are likely to be the same size, which makes for problems.

The solution was found in the twelfth century. How long is a yard? Originally, it was the pace of a man walking. King Henry I of England, according to legend, understood that such a yard was open to dispute, and decreed, therefore, that a yard would henceforth be the distance from the tip of his nose to the end of his royal thumb. Everyone could agree on that—and if not, off with their heads. King Henry, in his wisdom, created a yard that was standardized and fair for all.

When your child measures with pennies, beans, and batteries, he takes a mini-trip through the history of measurement. Like King Henry, he'll begin to grasp the need for a common standard for measuring.

So take out those pennies, paper clips, and kidney beans and start measuring the length of your telephone, sneakers, bananas, and lunch box. A bean or two may get lost under the refrigerator. But the concept of measurement will slowly sink in. The value of *that* is impossible to measure.

Bring out a centimeter ruler and let your child run his eyes and fingers over the tiny markings, the tinier markings, and the markings that are tinier still. Let the child get a feel for the length of one centimeter, two centimeters, three, and four. And when the child is comfortable with the ruler and has a sense for centimeters, then you're ready for HOW LONG?

Tell your child to close his eyes while you draw a line, using the ruler, four centimeters long. When you're done, the child opens his eyes and tries to guess the length of the line.

How close was his estimate? Let him use the ruler to find out. Now the tables turn. You shut your eyes, your child draws, you guess the length of the line, and the two of you compare your guess with the actual measurement.

Next round, make a change. Challenge your child to draw a line that's as close to three centimeters as possible—without using the ruler. After he draws, measure. How close did he get? Your turn to tackle the same task. How close to three centimeters did you get?

Here's another change. Take any object in the room that's *shorter* than your ruler—a paper clip, for instance—and ask your child to guess its length. After he guesses, compare his estimate with an actual measurement. Next time around, let your child pick an object for you to guess.

GRADES

first, second, and third

MATERIALS

paper
pencil
centimeter ruler
inch ruler

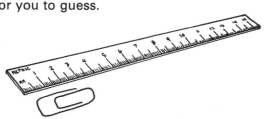

Don't be surprised if, after a while, your child's estimates are more accurate than your own. There's nothing about being a grown-up that gives you an advantage in estimating centimeters. But don't be upset if your child stumbles either. Measurement and estimation—the two skills required by this modest little game—are vast complexities, which everyone learns at his own pace.

What about inches? Clearly, you can play this game just as easily with an inch ruler. Remember, however, your child is growing up in a world more and more dominated by metric measurements. It's wise, therefore, to make centimeters his first measurement language. Then you can throw in that soon-to-be-outmoded unit, the inch, for a sort of bilingual enrichment.

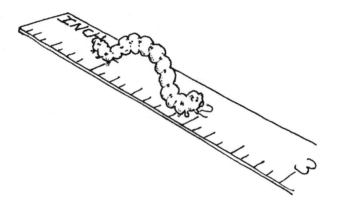

You measure length with a ruler, but you measure capacity with containers, which is a less elegant method and can, indeed, prove confusing. Ordinary English measures include gallons, quarts, pints, cups, tablespoons, and teaspoons. Then there are metric measures like liters and milliliters. Mindboggling! But you and your child have no choice: gallons and liters will always be a part of life, and must be mastered sooner or later.

The best and most delicious way for a child to learn more about these measures is to cook good food. And with the right recipes, you can make delectable delicacies in ten minutes or less. Here, then, are four of the right recipes for ten-minute temptations. The first two call for English measure, the system that probably feels most familiar to you. The second two call for metric measure. You can buy metric measuring cups and spoons in most stores these days. If you can't find such modern utensils, however, it's easy enough to mark your old measuring tools with a metric scale.

250	milliliters equals 1 cup
125	milliliters equals ½ cup
80	milliliters equals ⅓ cup
60	milliliters equals ¼ cup
15	milliliters equals 1 tablespoon
5	milliliters equals 1 teaspoon
2.5	milliliters equals ½ teaspoon
1.25	milliliters equals ¼ teaspoon

Then it's into the kitchen, and the pouring and ladling begins.

Peanut Butter Balls (makes 10 balls)

You need:

> ¾ cup raisin bran cereal
> ½ cup peanut butter
> 2 tablespoons powdered sugar

1. Crush the raisin bran with your fingers or with a spoon.
2. Mix together the raisin bran, peanut butter, and 1 tablespoon powdered sugar.
3. Form the mixture into small balls.
4. Coat the balls with the remaining powdered sugar.

Sweet Walnuts

You need:

> 1 cup shelled walnuts
> 2 tablespoons honey
> 2 tablespoons sugar
> waxed paper

1. Preheat oven to 300°.
2. Mix the walnuts, honey, and sugar. Make sure the walnuts are completely coated.
3. Spread the walnuts out on a cookie tray.
4. Bake at 350° for 8 to 10 minutes.
5. Put the hot walnuts on waxed paper to cool.
6. You can eat the nuts as soon as they have cooled, or you can put them in the refrigerator to chill.

Banana Cinnamon Shake (makes one glass)

You need:

    1 ripe banana
    250 ml milk
    2.5 ml vanilla
    15 ml honey
    2.5 ml cinnamon
    a jar with a lid

1. Mash the banana.
2. Mix all the ingredients in a jar.
3. Shake the jar vigorously.

Apple Pear Waldorf Salad (makes 2 large servings)

You need:

    250 ml diced red apple
    125 ml diced peeled pear
    60 ml shelled chopped walnuts
    15 ml shelled sunflower seeds
    15 ml raisins
    125 ml diced celery
    15 ml lemon juice
    2.5 ml sugar
    60 ml mayonnaise

1. Mix all the ingredients in a large bowl.

The floor may now be a swamp of honey and mayonnaise, delightfully stenciled with sneaker marks, but take comfort. The more your floor suffers, the more your child is gaining a familiarity with cups and milliliters.

chapter 10

Multiplication and Division

The five activities in this chapter will not only help your child understand multiplication and division, which is hard enough, but will also help your child memorize the crucial 231 multiplication and division problems that make up the dreaded table. Memorizing the multiplication table is an onerous task that is usually achieved with flash cards and drill. But—here's the good news—games can help too. In fact, according to a recent study, games can be just as effective as boring flash cards. I like that study, and so should you. It means you can play games, have fun, and help your child master the tables at the same time.

COUNT YOUR POINTS is a card game that makes multiplication as easy as a dot and a line. THAT GOONEY FAMILY FROM OUTER SPACE gets children multiplying to solve extraterrestrial problems. NUMBER DRAWING is a mathematical art activity. THE OUTSIDERS will help your child understand division problems with remainders. THREE-FOR-ALL takes three games from Chapter 8: Addition and Subtraction and transforms them into multiplication and division activities.

*C*OUNT YOUR POINTS

OUNT YOUR POINTS is a card game. It's fast. It's simple. It shows children how multiplication works. There are not many better games in the world of teaching than COUNT YOUR POINTS.

The first time Diana and I played, she helped me get the game ready. Together we picked out all the Aces, Twos, Threes, Fours, and Fives from a deck of cards. In this game, Aces equal one. Then I shuffled this mini-deck and said, of course, "Pick a card, any card." She picked a Four. That meant she had to draw four parallel vertical lines on a sheet of paper, like this:

GRADES

first, second, and third

MATERIALS

paper
pencil
a deck of cards (picture cards and Jokers removed)

I pointed to the deck again, and she picked a second card. It was a Three. I told her to draw three parallel horizontal lines crisscrossing the verticals, like this:

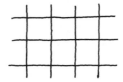

Then I told her to highlight the points of intersection between the two sets of lines.

She counted the points. There were twelve. Twelve, therefore, was her score.

My turn next. I reshuffled the deck and picked a card for myself. It was an Ace, so I drew one line.

I picked again—another Ace.

I highlighted the intersecting point.

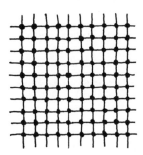

My score: one. A sorry showing!

Diana was overjoyed. Her delight didn't subside when I told her that you must win five rounds in order to be a COUNT YOUR POINTS champ. So we shuffled our cards and started round two.

Why limit the game to the numbers one (Ace) through five? Because I didn't want to overwhelm Diana with huge numbers in our first COUNT YOUR POINTS competition. On subsequent days, we did play with larger numbers. Eventually we played with Aces through Tens. The highest possible score then was one hundred.

Diana made a big mathematical discovery while we played. She already knew that combining three and five gives you eight. COUNT YOUR POINTS showed her a way to combine three and five and end up with fifteen. This was something new. How did this happen? Instead of combining a set of three with a set of five she was really making three groups (or rows) with five dots in each row. That's 5 and 5 and 5 or, putting it another way, that's 3 times you have 5.

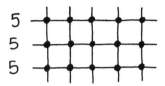

Why, that's multiplication. It's multiplication without symbols and without terminology, but multiplication nonetheless.

A year later, Diana was struggling to master the times tables. Occasionally, she'd forget a fact: for instance, seven times six. When that happened, I showed Diana how COUNT YOUR POINTS can help. I told her to draw seven vertical lines, crisscrossed by six horizontal lines, and count her points.

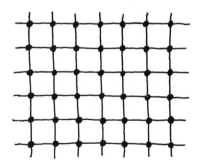

Answer? Forty-two.

Multiplication still wasn't easy. But at least she had a fail-safe way of getting the correct answers.

THAT GOONEY FAMILY FROM OUTER SPACE

Here is a Gooney from the planet Goon:

A Gooney has one eye, two mouths, no nose, and two ears. He has three arms with one hand on each arm and two fingers on each hand. A Gooney has one leg and two feet. Aside from that, he's just like you and me.

Gooneys live in families. This particular Gooney has a mother, a father, and a sister. That's four Gooneys altogether.

Time to figure out facts about this family. First, how many mouths are there in the Gooney family?

You can answer this question in two ways. You can draw a whole family and then count mouths:

or you can use a tally system. Make a box for each member of the family. Draw two slashes in each box representing mouths. Count the slashes. Younger children can count each slash. Older children will skip count two by two. Still older children will notice that this is four groups of two, or 4 × 2.

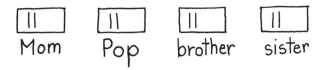

Mom   Pop   brother   sister

Time for a new problem. How many fingers are in the Gooney family? Again, you can draw the family and count the fingers, or make new boxes for a new tally.

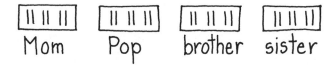

Mom   Pop   brother   sister

Younger children will count each finger. Older children will skip count by six. And the oldest of all will notice that there are four groups of six, or 4 × 6, making 24.

Then it's on to the Gooney family's ears, noses, and feet.

How about a new and much more complicated Gooney? Here she is:

This Gooney lives with her identical twin sister. With a bit of work you can figure out how many noses, fingers, ears, and eyes the twins have between them. You'll be amazed at the vastness of the sums.

There's no reason not to be creative in this game. In fact, the more creative you are in devising a Gooney and its family, the more amazing will be the game, and the more happily your child will go about the tasks of counting, skip counting, and—finally!—multiplying.

It was the end of second grade for Anna, and her classroom teacher was beginning to teach multiplication. Anna had already played a number of games like COUNT YOUR POINTS and THAT GOONEY FAMILY FROM OUTER SPACE that helped prepare her for the large new topic. So multiplication, as a concept, was not too difficult for her to understand.

Still, with Anna, there was reason for concern. Rote memorization was her nemesis. Sooner or later—in third grade, to be exact—she would have to memorize the multiplication table, and that was going to be no end of trouble. So I decided to give her a head start.

Think of the twos table—two, four, six, eight, ten, twelve, fourteen, sixteen, eighteen, twenty. The table is an exercise in skip counting by twos. When you multiply 2 × 3 you skip count by twos three times: two, four, six. Just so with every table. To solve 6 × 4 you skip count by sixes four times: six, twelve, eighteen, twenty-four. Children who can skip count by two, threes, fours, fives, and so on to tens have, in fact, mastered all the multiplication problems that must be memorized. I could have drilled Anna on skip counting by making her recite the words over and over. But NUMBER DRAWING was fun—and served the same purpose.

To start the game, I took a blank sheet of paper and announced that I was about to create a skip-counting drawing.

"For this drawing, I'm going to count by fours from four to forty. Every time I write a number, I'll put a dot beside it. I'm going to scatter the numbers all over the page."

GRADES

second and third

MATERIALS

paper
pencil
crayons

12
·

32
·

·8

·20

28·

·
24

·
16

·40

4·

·
36

"Now I'll connect the dots. I'll start at four, draw a line to eight, and then to twelve. When I get to forty, though, I'll be at the end, and I'll link that last dot with the first one."

While I drew from dot to dot I recited the fours table: "Four, eight, twelve, sixteen, twenty, twenty-four, twenty-eight, thirty-two, thirty-six, forty. That's the end. Now back to number four."

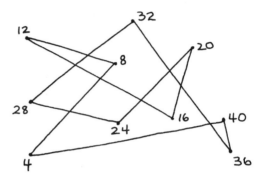

It made a nice design. Then I took out a crayon box and started to fill in different sections of the drawing in different colors. By the time I'd added a bit of red and yellow to the page, Anna said, "Oh, that's pretty. Can I make a drawing?"

"Sure," I answered. "You just have to pick a number from two to ten for skip counting. Which number do you want?"

"Can I do four?" she asked.

"That was my number! Maybe next time. Why don't you pick something different? Don't worry, I'll help you with the counting."

"Okay, I'll do three," she said.

"Good. That means you start with three and end at thirty."

Anna was ready to begin. She picked up her pencil. In the middle of a blank sheet of paper, she wrote the number three and placed a dot alongside. Six and a dot went in the left-hand corner of the page. Then she was stuck. She didn't know what number to put next.

"Count three more than six and you'll have it," I told her.

"Seven, eight, nine," she said. And she wrote the nine.

She kept counting until she reached thirty. Then she connected her dots, and colored her picture.

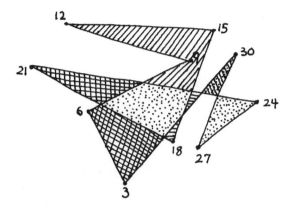

Anna liked her drawing. When I announced that she'd actually been practicing her threes table in multiplication, she beamed with pride.

Over the next months, Anna and I did a lot of NUMBER DRAW-ING. In time, she became a skillful skip counter. She memorized several multiplication tables that way, she got a good start on the others, and she did a lot of coloring, besides. She enjoyed herself, and so did I. I knew that when she got to third grade, arithmetic was going to be a little less hard than it might have been.

THE OUTSIDERS

GRADES

second and third

MATERIALS

paper
pencil

*T*his quick and easy game helps children understand division with remainders. To play, you and your child each pick a number between ten and thirty. Let's say you pick twelve and your child selects twenty-eight. Now you must draw twelve X's on a paper while your child draws twenty-eight X's on another sheet.

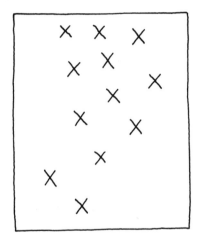

Next, you and your child both make fists with your right hands. You both call out the word "Once" while simultaneously shaking your fists in the air. Say "Twice" and shake your fists again. Say "Thrice" and shake your fists a third time. Finally, you shout out "Shoot." On "Shoot," you each extend (or "shoot") some fingers. You can shoot from one finger to all five. Let's say you shoot two fingers and your child shoots five. You add the fingers together. In this case, you have seven.

With this sum in mind, you each attack your paper of X's, and group your X's into sets of seven. When finished, you have one group of seven and five X's remaining. Your child has four groups of X's with none remaining. Who is the winner? Not the person with the most sets of X's, but the person with the *least* number of X's outside a set.

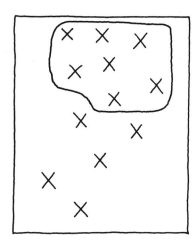

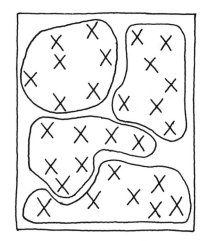

Your Paper   Your Child's Paper

In this round, your child wins. If you like the game, play again. The game champion must win two out of three rounds. You ought to be able to declare a victor in less than ten minutes. If you're waiting for food in a restaurant, that should be just about right.

Sometimes children will have trouble grouping X's. They may miscount. They may wind up with seven stray X's that can't easily be looped into a group. There are two solutions to such a problem. Solution one: you can erase badly located X's and redraw them in more convenient spots. Solution two: draw the X's in ink and draw the loops that surround groups in pencil. That way, you can redraw the loops, if problems arise, without disrupting the X's.

You can vary the game by increasing the range for starting X's. The game works well up to a maximum of one hundred X's. It will take a little longer to play with big numbers, but if you've got fifteen minutes to spare, why not?

THREE-FOR-ALL

GRADE

third

MATERIALS

paper
pencil
a deck of cards (picture cards
and Jokers removed)

With a nip here and a tuck there, three games introduced in Chapter 8 to teach addition and subtraction can be altered to help your child master multiplication and division. The three games are TIC-TAC-TOE, WAR, and NUMBER STORIES. Here they are, with new rules to fit the new situation.

Tic-Tac-Toe

This is a multiplication and division TIC-TAC-TOE board:

$$
\begin{array}{c|c|c}
9 \div 3 & 6 \times 2 & 15 \div 5 \\
\hline
4 \div 2 & 6 \times 3 & 7 \times 3 \\
\hline
18 \div 3 & 1 \times 4 & 10 \div 2
\end{array}
$$

Each box in the grid is filled with a multiplication or division problem. To play the game, you follow the rules for any game of TIC-TAC-TOE. Before you can write your X or O over a math problem in the grid, however, you must answer the arithmetic problem written there. Do you want an X in the middle? Then you must solve the problem 6 × 3. Do you want an O in the upper-right-hand corner? Then you must solve the problem 15 ÷ 5. If your child has trouble solving a problem, if he can't remember the answer or figure it out on his own, then tell him the correct solution.

Each time you play, make a new TIC-TAC-TOE board. You can use new problems or replay old ones. Here's a list of the 231 multiplication and division problems that your child needs to memorize. They should keep you busy for a while.

Multiplication

0×0	1×0	2×0	3×0	4×0	5×0	6×0	7×0	8×0	9×0	10×0
0×1	1×1	2×1	3×1	4×1	5×1	6×1	7×1	8×1	9×1	10×1
0×2	1×2	2×2	3×2	4×2	5×2	6×2	7×2	8×2	9×2	10×2
0×3	1×3	2×3	3×3	4×3	5×3	6×3	7×3	8×3	9×3	10×3
0×4	1×4	2×4	3×4	4×4	5×4	6×4	7×4	8×4	9×4	10×4
0×5	1×5	2×5	3×5	4×5	5×5	6×5	7×5	8×5	9×5	10×5
0×6	1×6	2×6	3×6	4×6	5×6	6×6	7×6	8×6	9×6	10×6
0×7	1×7	2×7	3×7	4×7	5×7	6×7	7×7	8×7	9×7	10×7
0×8	1×8	2×8	3×8	4×8	5×8	6×8	7×8	8×8	9×8	10×8
0×9	1×9	2×9	3×9	4×9	5×9	6×9	7×9	8×9	9×9	10×9
0×10	1×10	2×10	3×10	4×10	5×10	6×10	7×10	8×10	9×10	10×10

Division

0÷1	0÷2	0÷3	0÷4	0÷5	0÷6	0÷7	0÷8	0÷9	0÷10
1÷1	2÷2	3÷3	4÷4	5÷5	6÷6	7÷7	8÷8	9÷9	10÷10
2÷1	4÷2	6÷3	8÷4	10÷5	12÷6	14÷7	16÷8	18÷9	20÷10
3÷1	6÷2	9÷3	12÷4	15÷5	18÷6	21÷7	24÷8	27÷9	30÷10
4÷1	8÷2	12÷3	16÷4	20÷5	24÷6	28÷7	32÷8	36÷9	40÷10
5÷1	10÷2	15÷3	20÷4	25÷5	30÷6	35÷7	40÷8	45÷9	50÷10
6÷1	12÷2	18÷3	24÷4	30÷5	36÷6	42÷7	48÷8	54÷9	60÷10
7÷1	14÷2	21÷3	28÷4	35÷5	42÷6	49÷7	56÷8	63÷9	70÷10
8÷1	16÷2	24÷3	32÷4	40÷5	48÷6	56÷7	64÷8	72÷9	80÷10
9÷1	18÷2	27÷3	36÷4	45÷5	54÷6	63÷7	72÷8	81÷9	90÷10
10÷1	20÷2	30÷3	40÷4	50÷5	60÷6	70÷7	80÷8	90÷9	100÷10

Multiplication War

To play multiplication WAR, you need a deck of cards with all the picture cards and Jokers removed. Then you divide the deck evenly between you and your child.

The game begins when you and your child each take the two top cards from your respective decks and place them face up on the table.

Then you multiply the numbers on your own two cards and your child multiplies the numbers on his.

The player with the larger answer wins all four cards.

If the answers are the same,

WAR is declared.

Take three cards from your deck and place them face down on the table. Take two more cards and place them face up. Your child does this also. You and your child multiply your new face-up cards. The larger answer wins all fourteen cards in the playing field.

And the game goes on until one person captures all the cards and wins the WAR.

Number Stories

A NUMBER STORY is a tale you tell your child that is filled with arithmetic problems for the child to solve—not just addition and subtraction problems, but multiplication and division problems too. Here are two math-filled examples you can use.

Petunia Cat was very unhappy. She lived in a big house. The house had six rooms. There were five mice in each room. *(How many mice were in the house?)* But these were pet mice. They lived in cages, and Petunia wasn't allowed to bother them. There were three birds in each room. *(How many birds were in the house?)* But these were pet birds, and Petunia wasn't allowed to

chase them. Petunia wished she could go outside. There were five trees outside and in each tree lived four squirrels. *(How many squirrels lived in the trees?)* Petunia wished she could chase those squirrels. But she wasn't allowed out of the house. All Petunia ever got to eat was cat food. She got a can in the morning and a can at night. *(How many cans did she get in a week?)* Then a terrible thing happened. Petunia's human family adopted three kittens. The kittens played all day. They played three hours in the morning, four hours in the afternoon, and three hours at night. *(How many hours did the kittens play every day?)* Petunia went into the kitchen to get some peace and quiet. But the kittens followed her. Then Petunia and the three kittens saw twelve glasses of milk on the kitchen counter. All four jumped up on the counter and drank the milk. They each drank the same amount. *(How many glasses did they have each?)* As soon as they were finished, the humans came into the kitchen. "You bad cats, you drank all the milk," yelled the father. Then the father looked at Petunia. "Oh, Petunia. I know you didn't take any milk. It was those naughty kittens. You're a good cat, Petunia."

Petunia purred happily. Maybe it wasn't so bad having kittens in the house.

Megan was a witch. She loved casting magic spells. Every day she cast seven spells at noon and twelve spells at midnight. *(How many more spells did she cast at midnight?)* One day Megan was in a good mood. She saw five elves playing in the elf schoolyard. Each elf had a backpack. Megan cast a spell. She put four lollipops in each backpack. *(How many lollipops did Megan give the elves in all?)* Then she made a candy-cane fence out of forty-five candy canes. The elves shared the canes

equally. *(How many canes did each elf get?)* She made twenty-five raisin cookies for the elves. The elves shared them equally. *(How many cookies did each elf get?)*

The next day, Megan was in a bad mood. She saw the same five elves in the schoolyard. She didn't give them treats. Instead, she put four spiders in each of their backpacks. *(How many spiders did she put?)* She sent bad-smelling skunks to follow the elves home. Each elf was followed by seven skunks. *(How many skunks did Megan send after the elves?)* The elves liked it when Megan was in a good mood. They hated it when she was in a bad mood. So the elves went to Megan's sister, Bertha Witch. They asked Bertha to cast a spell that would put Megan in a good mood every single day. Bertha liked this idea. She cast the spell, and from then on it was lollipops and candy canes every day.

Now you can make up your own stories. Go ahead, just start talking. Don't worry about creating masterpieces of storytelling. There's something about homemade stories that fascinates children. Even the flimsiest adventure holds a child's interest, and his mathematical attention too. Why is this so? Why do cats like to lie down on paper? Some things just happen to be true, and there's no explaining why.

PART FOUR
OTHER SUBJECTS

chapter 11

Science

What attitudes should scientists bring to their work? Scientists should be curious. They should delight in asking questions. When Thomas Edison was a boy, he asked so many questions his father said, "Tom, all you are is one big question mark. I have a question mark for a son!"

Scientists should be ready for surprises. In 1882 Gideon Mantell, a British scientist, stumbled on a strange fossil. It looked like a huge iguana tooth. This remarkable discovery led Mantell to suggest that giant creatures used to roam the earth in prehistoric times. He called his creature an iguanodon and wrote the first scientific paper ever to describe dinosaurs. Dinosaurs were definitely a surprise.

Anton van Leeuwenhoek, who invented the first microscope, was surprised in the other direction. He peered into the microscope at a drop of water and was amazed to discover that tiny little creatures were swimming in it. Life is microscopic. Very surprising!

Scientists should be logical. They should enjoy figuring out why surprising facts exist. In 1931, an engineer named Karl Jansky tried to figure out why static gets in the way of radio communication. He eliminated all the known sources of static, yet he still heard noise. Where was the static from? Logic pointed to outer space. By investigating static, he opened a new field of scientific investigation: radio astronomy.

The best contribution you can make to your child's scientific education is to encourage these attitudes of mind: curiosity, readiness for surprise, a spirit of logical investigation. The four activities in this chapter can, in a small way, help. TAKE IT APART and WONDERINGS will help turn your own child into a scientific question mark. FAST AND FANTASTIC and GIANT BUBBLES will get the child conducting experiments. No disasters will occur, no atom bombs will blow up the garage. Yet your child may become a little more curious, alert, and eager to apply logic to mysterious phenomena.

Do you want still more science? Look at the list of read-aloud books in the Appendix. You'll find a collection of science books filled with experiments, explanations of scientific phenomena, and stories of animals, extinct and living, for you and your child to explore.

TAKE IT APART

What's inside a ballpoint pen? If you take one apart, will you discover something about how pens work?

What's inside a flower? If you take one apart, will you learn something about how flowers grow?

What's inside a candle? If you take one apart, will you understand more about why candles glow?

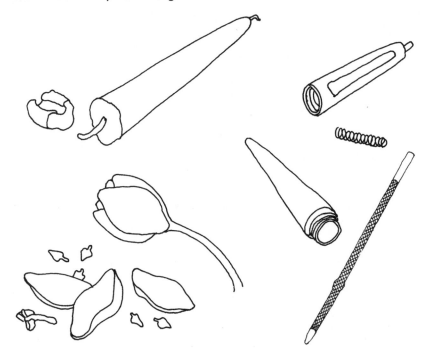

Tearing apart pens, flowers, and candles to find how they work isn't destruction; it's scientific investigation. That's why you should encourage a favorite childhood pastime—opening things up to see what's inside. Of course, you want to be careful about how you carry out these investigations, and on what.

Starting with *what*: What should you take apart? Plants and food are a good place to start. The next time you slice an apple, find out how many seeds it has. Then take apart a seed and see what's inside. Do all apples have the same number of seeds? Do the insides of all seeds look alike? Take apart a leaf and investigate the veins, the stem, and how it attaches to the plant.

Old toys are always good for a quick dismantling. Try taking apart a broken truck. Can you find out something about gears and wheels? Don't throw out that broken talking doll—dissect!

Sometimes it's worth taking apart something that works. Then you can try to put it back together again. Flashlights, for instance, are interesting to investigate.

How should you carry out investigations? Keep three points in mind. Point one: *be careful*. You may occasionally need a hammer or a screwdriver in order to decapitate a doll or disassemble a toy truck. You'll need a knife to cut open apples and oranges. Teach your child how to use these tools correctly. Make sure the child understands that he *must never* take things apart on his own. If he wants to investigate something new, he *must* ask permission first. Never open anything that makes you nervous. Use your good adult judgment. Don't mess with aerosol cans. Don't fool around with electricity. Keep away from glass objects. Your child's scientific knowledge will grow steadily and beautifully even if you limit your investigations to fruit, plants, and ballpoint pens.

Point two: scientific explorations can get messy. Digging up an old potted plant to examine the roots is a dirty job. It's best to wear old clothes for investigations and have plenty of paper towels around.

Point three: ask a lot of questions while you work.

"Why is a maple leaf shaped differently from an oak leaf?"

"Why is this wire here?"

"Whatever is the purpose of these little blue things?"

"Does every flower have these little stems?"

"Why are some pencil leads softer than others?"

"What gives ink its color?"

You don't need answers to your questions. The answers are less important than the questions themselves. Rather than accumulating facts, you want to establish a tone between you and your child, a tone of scientific inquiry.

WONDERINGS

Young children and scientists share a common trait: they're continually asking questions. "Why is the sky blue?" asks the young child. "How did the universe begin?" asks the scientist.

Unfortunately, some children lose their questioning curiosity about life and nature as they get older. These children lose their natural inclination toward science at the same time.

Is there any way to help children keep questioning? Often the companionship of an inquisitive adult—a living model of curiosity—is all a child needs to keep his mind filled with wonder. You can be this model for your child. What's required? Just ask lots of questions.

> How does a computer work?
> What makes a cat purr?
> Why does salty food make you thirsty?
> Where do fish sleep?
> When do fish sleep?

Asking questions about all you see and hear may feel strange. With a little practice, however, asking how, what, why, where, and when will feel perfectly natural.

Of course, you won't know the answers to your questions. Otherwise they wouldn't be honest questions. Occasionally you may decide to investigate. You might look in a book or ask a more informed friend. It's not necessary to get answers, however. What's important is observing the world and being curious. The point is to establish a good intellectual climate for your child. Don't worry about undermining your parental authority because you don't know the answers to questions. Children don't need their parents to know everything.

There is a certain type of question, however, that cries out to be answered: I-wonder-what-happens-if questions.

> I wonder what happens if you put sugar in water? Will it boil quicker than plain water?

I wonder what happens if you mix glue with green paint? Will you get green glue?

I wonder what happens if you put a plant in the closet? Will it grow without sunlight?

I wonder what happens if you let chocolate syrup dry out? Will you get chocolate sugar?

Surely you'll have to experiment with some of these wonder-ifs. Then, before you know it, your home will become a laboratory populated by questioning, investigating, curious scientists: you and your child.

FAST AND FANTASTIC

*H*ere are three quick, easy, and amazing science experiments that teachers love to use. You may love them too. If so, you will surely want to experiment some more. The list of read-aloud books in the Appendix includes some science books that are jam-packed with good experiments for first- through third-graders.

Experiment Number 1: Flying Pepper

Materials: salt, pepper, plastic spoon, plate

Have you ever mixed salt and pepper together by accident? Did you know that it's easy to separate them again? You need only a plastic spoon and the hair on your head. Prove it to yourself. Sprinkle a bit of salt on a plate. Mix in a pinch of pepper. Then take a plastic spoon. Rub the spoon in your hair for a second or two until the spoon is charged with static electricity. You'll know that the spoon is charged when your hair stands on end as you move the spoon away from your head.

Hold the spoon close to the salt and pepper, but don't let it touch the mixture. Watch while the pepper flies up to the spoon. The salt will stay on the plate.

Why does the pepper move? When you rub the plastic spoon in your hair, the spoon picks up a negative charge. The spoon will now attract anything that has a positive or a neutral charge (salt and pepper included). The salt, being heavier than pepper, however, can't fly off the plate so quickly. So the pepper pops up, and the salt sits still. Hold the spoon lower, and the salt will leap up also.

Experiment Number 2:
Catch That Dollar Bill

Materials: a dollar bill

I found this novel experiment in *Magic Science Tricks* by Dinah Moché. I've used it many times since. It amazes children and adults alike. I hope it will amaze experimenters in your house.

Have your child hold his hand like this:

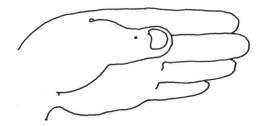

Now you hold a dollar bill between his thumb and fingers. Your child's fingers must not touch the dollar bill.

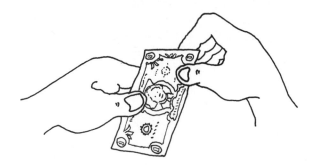

Inform your child that at any moment you will drop the dollar. You won't give him any warning before doing so. Dare your child to grab the bill. Sounds easy, right? It's not. Suddenly drop the bill. It will fall through the child's fingers before his brain receives the message to grab. Gravity—it's faster than the brain. What a force!

Experiment Number 3:
Rocket Bottle

Materials: empty clean wine bottle, cork from the bottle, ½ cup water, ½ cup vinegar, ⅓ cup baking soda, ¼ sheet of paper towel

You should perform this particular experiment outdoors or in some other wide open area—a spacious living room with high ceilings, for instance.

Pour the vinegar and water into the bottle.

Pour the baking soda onto the ¼ sheet of paper towel. Roll up the towel.

Drop the paper towel with the baking soda into the bottle. Secure the cork in the bottle.

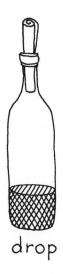

drop

cork

Now stand back. In a little bit, the cork will shoot out of the bottle.
Kaboom!

Why does this happen? The vinegar and baking soda combine
to create carbon dioxide gas. As more gas forms, pressure builds
up in the bottle. Finally there is enough pressure for the bottle to
pop its cork. This experiment is, of course, thrilling to behold.

pop

GIANT BUBBLES

GRADES

first, second, and third

MATERIALS

liquid detergent
length of strong string
two plastic straws
a pail of water

Enrico Fermi, the brainy physicist who ushered in the nuclear age, liked to play with spinning tops when he was little. Motion intrigued him. How did the tops stay upright? Fermi was filled with wonder. He investigated. Eventually he came to an original and unique understanding of this phenomenon and developed a theory of the gyroscope. From a young boy fascinated with a child's toy, Fermi developed into one of the major scientists of our era. Might GIANT BUBBLES produce a Fermi reaction in your own child? A Fermi reaction, in this case, would mean the development of so much interest in bubbles that your child will want to learn more and more about how the bubbles work. Investigation and study might result. Scientific curiosity might grow. But even if not, you and your child will certainly have a few bubbly minutes of fun.

You can make GIANT BUBBLES inside your house, but be prepared for a mess. Work in the kitchen, bathroom, or some other area where a wet, soapy floor is acceptable. Be ready with a mop for cleanup. A yard, park, or roof might be the best bet, though.

Before you start, you need a frame. Cut about five feet of strong string and thread it through two plastic straws. Then tie the ends of the string in a knot.

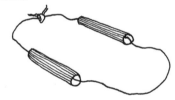

Now you need bubble solution. Fill your pail with ten cups of water. Mix in a cup of detergent, maybe a little more.

That's it. You're prepared. Hold the frame by the straws and dip it into the bubble solution. Lift the frame gently. Let the excess liquid drip. Then gently wave the frame in the air. A large luminescent bubble should appear. If there is no bubble, dip again. It may take a little practice, but bubbles will soon enough be floating through the air. You may want to experiment with your bubbles. What happens if you blow into the frame? What happens if you wave the frame very slowly? What happens if you change the size of the frame? What happens if you add more water to the solution? What happens if you add more detergent? What happens if you cut the straws to tiny bits? A few minutes of scientific experimentation and you'll find out.

It takes only ten minutes to get excited about this activity, but most children will be happy to play for hours. If several children are playing, you'll want at least one bubble frame for each. Bubble-making is a fine way to lighten and brighten any outdoor birthday party or picnic. And if some young partygoers happen to ask where bubbles come from, simply say: "Bubbles, my dears, come from the natural surface tension of the water, broken up slightly by the addition of soap. This allows the bubble to form. Look quick! Here comes a big one!"

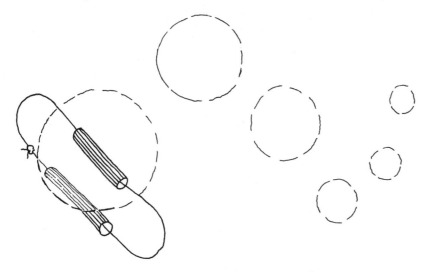

chapter 12

Social Studies

Everybody agrees that large numbers of junior high and high school students are sadly ignorant about geography, history, and current events. Many young adults have trouble, according to one alarming study, identifying the United States on an unmarked map. They don't know about the Second World War. They have never heard of Stalin. It's a terrible situation. But what to do about this ignorance? Should we have a national curriculum that outlines all the social studies topics every child in the United States should master between first and twelfth grade? Should children be given lists of facts and dates to memorize? Should we stress ethnic history? Should children study one topic in depth or many topics in a more superficial fashion? Everyone disagrees—which is no help.

Teachers do tend to agree, however, on one thing. If a child comes to school already knowing a lot about the world, if the child is interested in events and cultures past and present, if the child finds news and maps and governments interesting—that child will usually do well in social studies, regardless of the specific classroom approach to the subject. Parents, in short, can help.

There are five activities in this chapter. The first, GO FIGHT CITY HALL, offers your child a way to get involved in government. The second, TO TELL THE TRUTH, helps your child learn about history, civics, current events, anthropology, and sociology while playing a simple trivia game. WORLD TAGS is a novel way to study geography in your kitchen. WRITING EGYPTIAN will help your child imagine the world of the ancient Egyptians by teaching him to write in hieroglyphics. The last project, TIME CAPSULE, will send you and your child on an imaginary voyage into the future.

The activities in this chapter will trigger your child's curiosity about the news of the day, about foreign cultures, about history, about the world. Curiosity is good. Encourage it!

GO FIGHT CITY HALL

GRADES

first, second, and third

MATERIALS

paper
pencil
envelope
postage stamp

When I was in second grade—many centuries ago—the teacher gave our class a wonderful assignment. We had to think about our city. We had to think of one special thing that we liked about the city, one thing that we thought needed changing in the city, and one question about how the city works. With these three thoughts in mind, we all wrote letters to government officials. Some of us wrote the mayor. Some of us wrote City Council members. Some of us wrote our city's members of Congress. Some wrote to our city representatives in the state legislature. Some wrote the governor. One person even wrote the president.

A few weeks later, replies began pouring in. There was terrific excitement each day as we tore open letters from various officials. Mostly we got form letters thanking us for our interest. A few of us, however, received thoughtful replies. Of course, some disappointed people didn't get answers at all. Our teacher warned us that might happen.

I never forgot this lesson. I never forgot the excitement my classmates and I felt as we read our letters. Years later, when I became a teacher myself, I used this same assignment in my classes. I saw, now from a teacher's point of view, how special this letter writing is for children. All my students were affected to some degree by this experience. Every child gained some insight into how government works. Every child learned that government should be responsive to citizen concerns and complaints.

You can start your child on this civic path with a single letter. The next time your child complains about garbage on the streets, compliments a new playground, expresses concern over pollution, or wonders how a person becomes mayor, grab a pencil and paper.

Perhaps your child wants to tell public officials his ideas but balks at writing. Then, let him dictate his letters to you. Once he has the dictated version, he can copy it in his own hand or just sign it and send it off.

How do you get addresses? Most phone books carry listings for local officials. You can write senators and congresspeople in Washington. The address is: United States Congress, Washington, D.C.,

20510. The president lives at The White House, 1600 Pennsylvania Avenue, Washington, D.C., 20500.

You can write other interesting, though less obvious, officials: your local police commissioner, fire commissioner, sanitation commissioner, or transportation chief. At the national level, you might write the Secretary of Labor, the Secretary of Education, or the Secretary of the Treasury. Telephone information in Washington, D.C., will supply the necessary addresses.

More people live in China than in any other country on earth. True? False?

Texas is the largest state in the United States. True? False?

When Abraham Lincoln went to school, every classroom had a computer. True? False?

The United States once went to war against Japan, Germany, and Italy at the same time. True? False?

These questions are easy for you to answer, but they might prove tricky for your child. That's why asking such questions makes a good game—sort of a beginner's Trivial Pursuit. There's no reason to keep track of right or wrong answers. There's no set number of questions you need ask. The game is a good way to pass time while waiting on movie lines or shopping at the supermarket. The more you play, the more information your child will pick up.

Children love compiling information. They want to know about their world. They're fascinated by different cultures, by history, by what life was like when you were little. They don't want to hear lectures on these subjects, however. They're unlikely to sustain interest in any one topic for very long. Instead, most children like collecting a fact here and a fact there.

Don't expect your child to remember every fact. It's likely, however, that some facts will be more interesting and memorable to your child than others—and you never know which ones these special facts will be. If you focus a lot of attention on facts relating to World War II, your child may thread this information together. He'll begin creating mental pictures of that time.

Once you get into the habit, it's easy to think of TO TELL THE TRUTH questions. You can ask questions about history, ancient or modern:

In ancient times, warriors fought with bows, arrows, and spears, not with guns. True? False?

Scientists in ancient Greece invented the atom bomb. True? False?

TO TELL THE TRUTH

GRADES

second and third

You can ask political questions:

In the United States, we vote for our presidents every four years. True? False?

The president makes all the laws. True? False?

Every state in the United States has its own government. True? False?

You can ask questions about different countries and cultures:

In Holland people speak Hollandish. True? False?

Eskimos eat whale blubber. True? False?

When it's lunchtime in New York, it's lunchtime everywhere in the world. True? False?

When you play, make sure to include some questions with obvious answers:

George Washington played in a rock 'n' roll band. True? False?

When I was a little girl, dogs and cats could talk. True? False?

In Florida, no one ever eats oranges. True? False?

Children love such questions. The silliness is fun, and it feels good to be so sure of the answers.

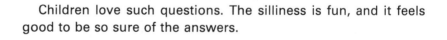

WRITING EGYPTIAN

Would your child like to write in Egyptian hieroglyphics? It's not that hard to do. The ancient Egyptians used a phonetic code in their writing. They didn't include every letter sound that we need in English—but you can make substitutions, or leave out a sound or two. Here's a chart of Egyptian sounds and symbols:

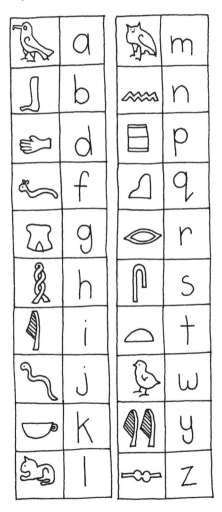

How do you write *Cleopatra* in Egyptian? You must pay attention to the sounds and not the letters in the words. Since there is no *o* in the Egyptian alphabet, leave that sound out.

K   L   P   A   T   R   A

Try writing your own name, your child's name, your pet's name. Try writing sentences. How about an Egyptian WELCOME sign for your front door? Or an Egyptian DO NOT ENTER sign for your child's bedroom door?

Writing in hieroglyphics is a wonderful way to interest children in ancient cultures. Learning hieroglyphics gives children a subtle lesson about culture too. Although it's true that ancient Egyptians lived very differently than we do today, there are important ways in which we are all alike. The Egyptians could read and write. They recorded their stories, history, and ideas, just as we do. It's good for children to see that societies can be different from one another but still have similarities.

The Egyptians also had a number system based on ten, just like our number system, though with a few differences. You might try some Egyptian math, therefore, as well as writing. Here's how the system works. There is no digit for zero. You write the numbers 1 to 9 like this:

1	2	3	4	5	6	7	8	9

These are called staffs. The placement of the staffs makes no difference:

||| is 3, | (stacked) is 3, and || | is 3.

Here are the symbols for 10, 20, 30, and so on:

∩ ∩∩ ∩∩∩ ∩∩∩
10   20   30   40   50   60   70   80   90

These are called heel bones.
Hundreds are written like this:

? ?? ??? ??? ??? ??? ??? ??? ???
100 200   300   400   500   600   700   800   900

These are called scrolls.
Thousands, otherwise known as lotus flowers, look like this:

1,000

The symbol for every ten thousand is a pointing finger:

10,000

For a hundred thousand the ancient Egyptians drew a burbot fish:

100,000

And for a million, the symbol was an astonished person!

1,000,000

Here's how you put numbers together. For 15 you write:

∩ |||||

For 206 you write:

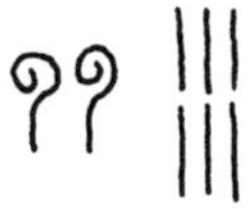

ℙℙ |||
   |||

For 3,167 you write:

𝒸 𝒸 𝒸 ℙ ∩∩∩ ||||
𝒴 𝒴 𝒴   ∩∩∩ |||

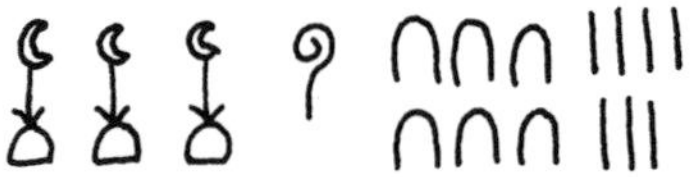

For 20,003 you write:

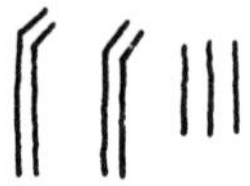

𝄖 𝄖 |||

For 1,111,111 you write:

𝕏 ↘ 𝄖 𝒴 ℙ∩ |

After you get the hang of writing numbers, try adding and sub-tracting. Here's an example:

$$\begin{array}{r} 32 \\ +\ 45 \\ \hline 77 \end{array}$$ is the same as

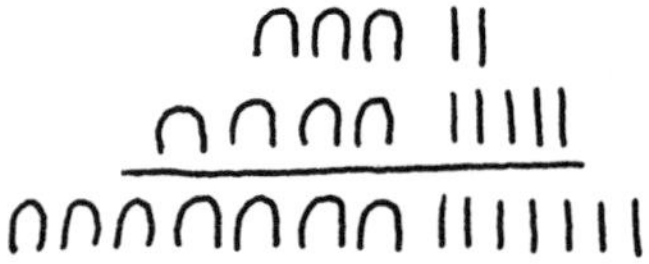

∩∩ ||
∩∩∩∩ |||||
_____
∩∩∩∩∩∩∩ |||||||

Here's another example:

$$\begin{array}{r} 35 \\ + 28 \\ \hline 63 \end{array}$$ is the same as

$$\begin{array}{l} \cap\cap\cap\; |||| \\ \cap\cap\; |||||||| \\ \hline \cap\cap\cap\; ||||| \\ \cap\cap\quad|\,|||| \\ \quad\quad ||| \end{array} = \begin{array}{l} \cap\cap\cap \boxed{\begin{array}{l}|||||\\|||||\end{array}} \\ \cap\cap \\ \quad ||| \end{array} = \begin{array}{l} \cap\cap\cap \\ \cap\cap\cap \\ \quad ||| \end{array}$$

This time after adding, I ended up with thirteen staffs. I had to exchange ten staffs, therefore, for one heel bone. Just the opposite situation can occur in subtraction. Sometimes you must exchange one heel bone for ten staffs to subtract correctly. The system is enough like our own to make it fairly easy for children to learn, and different enough to make it exotic and interesting.

WORLD TAGS

GRADES

second and third

MATERIALS

paper
pencil
thumbtacks or tape
scissors
a large map of the world

In my kitchen, you can find dishwashing detergent made in Ohio, cookies from Denmark, vinegar from France, olive oil from Italy, matches from Minnesota, cat food from California, juice from Florida, coffee from Colombia, syrup from Canada, tin foil from Virginia, a dish towel from India, and horseradish from Japan. My kitchen is an adventure in geography. Yours is too. If you look closely, you'll find that virtually everything that you buy, virtually everything that enters your house—food, clothes, furniture, electrical appliances—comes with some mark declaring its point of origin.

Here is a way to use dish towels and cat food to teach your child about geography. Get a big map of the world and place it on a wall. Then, as you buy things, take a look at the labels. Where does that soap come from? How about the tomato paste? What about that winter scarf? As soon as you find out the city, state, or country, write SOAP, TOMATO PASTE, or SCARF on a bit of paper, and tape or tack this paper tag onto the map. How long will it take you to have tags on every continent? How long will it take to have tags on every state in the U.S.A.? What states fill up with tags? What countries? What countries are tagless? Do some countries seem to specialize in food or clothes? Do some countries seem to export absolutely everything?

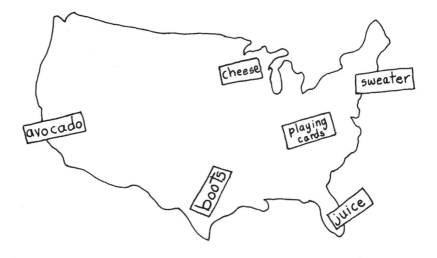

230

As you cover your map with tags, you may find that your child develops a special interest in one country or another. Take advantage. Make a quick trip to the library. Borrow books on Italy or China—books with plenty of pictures are best. Even if your child doesn't become a China expert, he'll still learn a lot. He'll become familiar with the map. In time, he'll probably recognize physically distinctive states like Texas and countries like Italy. He'll realize that his life in his hometown is connected to the lives of people in many towns and countries around the world.

TIME CAPSULE

GRADE

third

MATERIALS

a shoe box
(contents of the box will vary)

One way to help your child understand our world today is to start him thinking about what the world will be like in the future. How can you get your child thinking about life in, say, the year 2020? A shoe box transformed into a TIME CAPSULE can do the trick. The next time you buy a pair of shoes, keep the box. Explain to your child that you're going to fill this box with special objects. When the box is full, you will hide it deep in a closet or attic. The box will stay hidden for years and years. It will be a TIME CAPSULE. In the future, you will open the box and examine the treasures inside.

What should go into your capsule? What will be interesting ten, twenty, thirty years in the future? You'll surely want to include personal items. Perhaps there's a special birthday card or an A+ spelling test your child wants to save. Don't limit the contents to personal mementos, however. Instead, spend time talking with your child about things in our world today that may disappear in the future. Think about transportation. How do we get around today? We have cars, buses, planes, and trains. What will transportation be like in the new millennium? Will we have cars? Perhaps human fax machines will instantly send us wherever we want to go. If you believe this could happen, you might include a model car in the box.

How about food? Will there be fast-food restaurants? Maybe not. Maybe there will be machines, like today's cash machines, that dispense food on every street corner for diners on the run. If that's the case, you might want to add a Ronald McDonald doll to the box. If you don't have one at home, wait until your next trip to the Golden Arches and get one. Better yet, take a camera and photograph the McDonald's. Imagine your surprise thirty years from now when you see a photo of that strange-looking restaurant in your TIME CAPSULE shoe box.

Will we use money in the future? Perhaps the dollar bill will give way altogether to plastic credit cards. Discuss the possibility with your child. If he thinks that money is on the way out, he may want to include a dollar or two in the capsule.

How will you come up with ideas for the TIME CAPSULE? You

will think about all the important technological and sociological aspects of our lives today, and then try to imagine how these will change in the future. You'll think about food, transportation, health care, housing, government, the environment, clothes, recreation, entertainment, and how we get information. In order to fill the shoe box, you and your child will become sociologists of sorts.

Don't try to fill the shoe box up in one day. Leave it out for a while. As inspiration strikes, add a this or a that.

When the box is full, tape the lid in place and write the date on top. Then hide the box. No need to stop the collecting process, however. When your first box is full, start all over again with a new, ready-for-the-future shoe box.

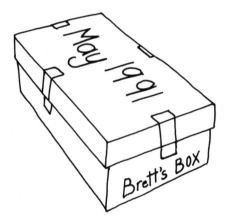

APPENDICES

A LIST OF IMPORTANT WORDS

In deciding which category to place a word, I've taken three points into consideration: (1) the intrinsic difficulty of the word; (2) how often the word appears in children's literature; (3) how early in a child's reading career he is likely to encounter the word. That's why the word *many*, which is used with great frequency and introduced in the earliest of beginning readers, is in the Beginning list, while *best*, a word just as easy to read, is in the Intermediate list.

Beginning Words

a	by	girl	I'll	oh
all	call	give	in	old
am	came	go	into	on
an	can	going	is	one
and	car	good	it	or
any	cat	got	jump	out
are	come	had	let	pig
as	cry	has	like	play
ask	day	hat	look	put
at	did	have	made	ran
ate	do	he	make	red
away	dog	help	man	ride
be	down	hen	many	run
bed	eat	her	me	sad
big	end	here	mouse	said
black	fat	him	must	saw
blue	find	home	my	say
book	fish	hot	new	see
boy	fly	house	no	she
brown	for	how	not	sit
bus	funny	I	now	slow
but	get	if	of	so

stop	then	top	we	yellow
sun	they	two	well	yes
tell	this	up	will	you
that	three	us	with	
the	to	walk	woman	
them	too	was	work	

Intermediate Words

add	coat	first	kitten	other
after	cold	five	knew	our
again	corn	floor	know	over
airplane	cow	food	land	people
along	cried	four	large	pick
also	cut	fox	last	place
answer	dark	friend	late	please
apple	doll	frog	laugh	pretty
baby	door	from	leg	pull
ball	drive	gave	light	puppy
barn	duck	goes	lion	queen
bear	easy	gone	little	rabbit
became	egg	green	live	read
become	elephant	happy	lost	real
bell	eve	hard	may	really
below	ever	hello	milk	right
bird	every	herself	miss	room
birthday	fall	hide	mother	seem
boat	family	himself	Mr.	set
box	far	horse	Mrs.	shop
cake	farm	hour	name	side
can't	fast	inside	next	sing
cap	father	it's	night	sleep
chair	feel	just	once	some
city	feet	keep	open	something
climb	fire	king	orange	sometime

soon	ten	town	want	while
start	thank	toy	wash	white
store	there	tree	way	who
street	thing	try	went	why
such	think	turn	were	your
table	time	under	what	zoo
take	took	use	when	
talk	top	very	where	

Hotshot Words

about	bread	end	heard	move
above	bring	enough	high	much
across	brother	even	hill	myself
against	buy	eye	hold	near
almost	carry	farmer	however	nest
always	change	field	hurt	never
animal	chicken	finally	idea	nose
another	children	flower	important	nothing
around	clean	follow	kind	often
back	close	found	later	only
basket	complete	full	learn	own
beautiful	country	garden	leave	paper
because	different	glad	left	part
been	does	goat	letter	party
before	done	grandfather	long	picture
began	don't	grandmother	lunch	piece
beginning	draw	grass	maybe	point
behind	drink	great	might	pony
being	during	grow	mind	problem
best	each	happen	money	question
better	early	hand	monkey	quickly
between	earth	head	more	rain
both	eight	hear	morning	reach

remember	show	teacher	usually	wood
ring	since	their	voice	word
river	sister	these	wagon	world
road	six	those	wait	would
round	small	thought	warm	write
school	squirrel	through	watch	yard
self	stay	today	water	year
seven	stick	together	which	yet
shall	still	train	window	young
sheep	study	true	wish	
shoe	sure	until	without	
should	surprise	upon	won't	

BOOKS FOR READING ALOUD

Here is a list of books that you may enjoy reading to your child. A good read-aloud book should have an exciting plot, be well written, hold the child's attention, and delight you, the adult, too. Some of the books here can be read in a single sitting. Others are chapter books that will need a week or more of bedtimes to complete. Sometimes you'll start a chapter book with high expectations but your child will become bored, or confused, or both. If this happens, there's only one thing to do. Stop reading the book and pick a different one for tomorrow night.

I've arranged the books in seven categories: fiction, fairy tales, poetry, social studies, science, math, and jokes. Whenever possible I've listed the books in order of difficulty, beginning with the easiest. But sometimes younger children are so enthusiastic about a book that they can follow complicated plots with delight and enthusiasm. So don't take that aspect of the list too literally.

Fiction

Caps for Sale by Esphyr Slobodkina
Cloudy with a Chance of Meatballs by Judith Barrett
Millions of Cats by Wanda Gag
Miss Nelson Is Missing by Harry Allard
The Story of Ferdinand by Munro Leaf
What Do You Say, Dear? by Sesyle Joslin
The Crack-of-Dawn Walkers by Amy Hest
Imogene's Antlers by David Small
Horton Hatches the Egg by Dr. Seuss
Winnie-the-Pooh by A. A. Milne
House at Pooh Corner by A. A. Milne
Stuart Little by E. B. White
Charlotte's Web by E. B. White
The Stories Julian Tells by Ann Cameron
Mrs. Piggle-Wiggle by Betty MacDonald
My Father's Dragon by Ruth Stiles Gannett

Little Bookroom by Eleanor Farjeon
Four Dolls by Rumer Godden
The Borrowers by Mary Norton
Half Magic by Edward Eager
Just So Stories by Rudyard Kipling
The Reluctant Dragon by Kenneth Grahame
Sarah, Plain and Tall by Patricia MacLachlan
The Animal Family by Randall Jarrell
The Gingerbread Rabbit by Randall Jarrell
The Enormous Egg by Oliver Butterworth
The Devil's Storybook by Natalie Babbitt
The Phantom Tollbooth by Norton Juster
Abel's Island by William Steig
The Amazing Bone by William Steig
The Real Thief by William Steig
Indian in the Cupboard by Lynne Reid Banks
Stories for Children by Isaac Bashevis Singer
The Chronicles of Narnia by C. S. Lewis
Harriet the Spy by Louise Fitzhugh
How to Eat Fried Worms by Thomas Rockwell
Harold and the Purple Crayon by Crockett Johnson
Alexander and the Terrible, Horrible, No Good, Very Bad Day by
    Judith Viorst
*My Mama Says There Aren't Any: Zombies, Ghosts, Vampires,
Creatures, Demons, Monsters, Fiends, Goblins, or Things* by
    Judith Viorst
Many Moons by James Thurber
Sam, Bangs and Moonshine by Evaline Ness
Crow Boy by Taro Yashima
Thy Friend, Obadiah by Brinton Turkle
Tell Me a Mitzi by Lore Segal
Old Mother West Wind by Thornton W. Burgess
The Houdini Box by Brian Selznick
Jacob Two-Two Hooded Fang by Mordecai Richler
Freckle Juice by Judy Blume
Rabbit Hill by Robert Lawson

Caddie Woodlawn by Carol Ryrie Brink
Mr. Popper's Penguins by Richard and Florence Atwater
The Adventures of Treehorn by Florence Parry Heide
The Secret Garden by Frances Hodgson Burnett
The 13 Clocks by James Thurber
The Witch of Fourth Street and Other Stories by Myron Levoy
The Cabin Faced West by Jean Fritz
The Half-a-Moon Inn by Paul Fleischman
The Cat Who Went to Heaven by Elizabeth Coatsworth

Fairy Tales and Mythology

The Classic Fairy Tales edited by Iona and Peter Opie
Black Folktales by Julius Lester
Jack Tales by Richard Chase
D'Aulaire's Book of Greek Myths by Ingri and Edgar Parin d'Aulaire
D'Aulaire's Norse Gods and Giants by Ingri and Edgar Parin d'Aulaire
Fairy Tales by e. e. cummings
The Juniper Tree and Other Tales from Grimm translated by Lore Segal and Randall Jarrell
American Tall Tales by Adrien Stoutenburg
It Could Always Be Worse by Margot Zemach
Why Mosquitoes Buzz in People's Ears: A West African Tale by Verna Aardema
The Girl Who Cried Flowers and Other Tales by Jane Yolen

Science

Giants of Land, Sea, and Air—Past and Present by David Peters
Sterling: The Rescue of a Baby Harbor Seal by Sandra Verrill White and Michael Filisky
Animals Do the Strangest Things by Leonora and Arthur Hornblow
Animal Fact/Animal Fable by Seymour Simon
Jupiter by Seymour Simon

Stars by Seymour Simon
Dr. Zed's Dazzling Book of Science Activities by Gordon Penrose
Mr. Wizard's Supermarket Science by Don Herbert
Magic Science Tricks by Dinah Moché
Science Experiments You Can Eat by Vicki Cobb
Bet You Can: Science Possibilities to Fool You by Vicki Cobb
   and Kathy Darling
Science Games and Puzzles by Laurence B. White, Jr.
The Magic School Bus: Inside the Human Body by Joanna Cole
Simple Science Experiments by Hans Jürgen Press
Sharks by Ann McGovern

Math

When Sheep Cannot Sleep by Satoshi Kitamura
Anno's Counting House by Mitsumasa Anno
How Much Is a Million? by David M. Schwartz
*The Biggest, Smallest, Fastest, Tallest Things You've Ever Heard
   Of* by Robert Lopshire
All in a Day by Mitsumasa Anno and others
Anno's Mysterious Multiplying Jar by Masaichiro and Mitsumasa
   Anno
Kids Are Natural Cooks by Roz Ault
The I Hate Mathematics! Book by Marilyn Burns
Math for Smarty Pants by Marilyn Burns

Social Studies

Mummies Made in Egypt by Aliki
Why Don't You Get a Horse, Sam Adams? by Jean Fritz
And Then What Happened, Paul Revere? by Jean Fritz
Cathedral: The Story of Its Construction by David Macaulay
Castle by David Macaulay
Wanted Dead or Alive: The Story of Harriet Tubman by Ann
   McGovern
Amos Fortune, Free Man by Elizabeth Yates

Story of Thomas Alva Edison, the Wizard of Menlo Park by
   Margaret Davidson
Make-Believe Empire by Paul Berman
Ben and Me by Robert Lawson
Mr. Revere and I by Robert Lawson

Poetry

When We Were Very Young by A. A. Milne
Now We Are Six by A. A. Milne
The Random House Book of Poetry for Children selected by Jack
   Prelutsky
All the Small Poems by Valerie Worth
Spin a Soft Black Song by Nikki Giovanni
Oh, What Nonsense edited by William Cole
Piping Down the Valleys Wild edited by Nancy Larrick
Sir Francis Drake: His Daring Deeds by Roy Gerrard
Sir Cedric by Roy Gerrard
*A Visit to William Blake's Inn: Poems for Innocent and
   Experienced Travelers* by Nancy Willard

Joke and Riddle Books

Bennett Cerf's Book of Riddles by Bennett Cerf
101 Bug Jokes by Katy Hall and Lisa Eisenberg
Haunted House Jokes by Louis Phillips
Jokes for Children by Marguerite Kohl and Frederica Young
More Jokes for Children by Marguerite Kohl and Frederica
   Young
Eight Ate: A Feast of Homonym Riddles by Marvin Terban

A NOTE TO TEACHERS

There are many occasions for teachers to use ten-minute activities in the classroom. Before starting a reading lesson, take a few minutes to warm the class up with a round of FLIP A DIP WITH A DRIP AND SLIP. When a math lesson ends early, spend the extra time telling NUMBER STORIES or playing a round of NUMBERBOW. When an art teacher is a few minutes late, or when your class is ready for assembly but assembly isn't ready for your class, play THE CLUB GAME. When a couple of children complete work in a flash, let them play ADDITION/SUBTRACTION TIC-TAC-TOE until the rest of the class finishes up.

Most *Games for Learning* are designed for two players, but with a bit of adjusting you can transform many games into whole-class or small-group events. Once your class is familiar with a game, you can assign pairs of children to play together—a fine alternative to worksheets. Here's a way to get individual attention for your students: arrange for fifth- or sixth-graders to come and play games with the children in your classroom.

Try recruiting parents to come to school and play games with individual children. Send home an invitation requesting one hour of parent time during the school year. Explain to your students that when Mom and Dad come to your class, they'll learn a simple game and then play it several times with different children.

You might enlist parental help in playing games at home. Is Joanne having trouble developing a sight vocabulary? Send home instructions for PYRAMID. Is Billy having trouble understanding place value? Send home instructions for TARGET.

How about a game night in school? Invite parents for an evening of cookies and game instruction. In an hour or so, you can teach a dozen games. Then parents can give their children some fun-filled academic help.

Parent-teacher conference time offers another occasion to teach games. When you tell Rose's parents about her problems with writing, you can suggest that TAKE A STORY or SILENT CONVERSATION might be good games to play at home.

In the classroom you can use games at four levels of instruction. First of all, you can introduce new topics with a game. Suppose you're about to tackle addition with exchange. Why not start with a game of COLLECT TEN? COLLECT TEN will lay the groundwork for exchanging ones for tens in a playful and concrete way. When the time comes to introduce the written form, your students will have a mental construct for the mathematical ideas. This will make the symbolic notation easier to remember.

Games also work well as coinstructional tools. Are your students learning short vowel sounds? Along with other approaches to the subject, try playing SWITCHEROO. You'll find that children concentrate very hard on the sounds for *a* and *i* when game points are at stake.

You probably already use games for drill and practice. Whenever your students must memorize word lists or addition and subtraction facts, games make the task more pleasing.

Finally, you can review old topics with a game. Has it been a while since your class worked with patterns? PATTERN GRIDS will remind your students of patterning in a delightful way. Does Jimmy need to review skip counting before going on to multiplication? Try playing DO IT BEFORE I COUNT TO . . .

Games for Learning covers a lot of territory. You will find something here that touches on most major academic topics in the kindergarten-through-third-grade curriculum. Because the book is organized by subject matter, you'll find it easy to locate the games you need. Here is a breakdown of skills that are addressed in the book.

Part One: Think About It

In *Chapter 1: The Hand, The Ear, The Eye*, you'll find games centered on motor and perceptual development. Some games help increase children's small motor control and hand-eye coordination. Other games foster strong auditory perception, including auditory discrimination, attentiveness, and memory. There are also games that exercise visual perception, including figure-ground relationships, visual discrimination, directionality, visual sequencing, spatial thinking, visualization, visual planning, and spatial analysis.

In *Chapter 2: Logical Thinking*, you'll find games that develop logical reasoning. There are games that help children define whole and part relationships; that promote the ability to classify and organize information in logical categories; that help children form subcategories; that lead to open-ended thinking; that develop youngsters' ability to find and isolate attributes; that foster children's ability to analyze and create patterns. Children who have strength in these areas usually have an agility of mind that makes all academic work easier.

Part Two: Read and Write

There are four language-arts chapters in Part Two. Teachers using any of the major methods to teach reading will find something useful here. Some games develop sight vocabulary. This is important for all young readers, but especially helpful in classrooms using controlled-vocabulary basal readers. Other activities develop phonetic decoding abilities. Many games are compatible with an experience or process approach to reading. All of the games can be used in conjunction with literature-based whole-language reading programs.

Chapter 3: Word Power focuses on both developing an emergent reader's excitement about the written word and strengthening a more advanced reader's sight vocabulary. Several of the games in this chapter refer to the List of Important Words in the Appendix. This list is compiled from the Dolch list of common sight words, the Dolch list of common nouns, and the Fry and Sakiey list of 3,000 words (Elizabeth Sakiey and Edward Fry, *3,000 Instant Words* [Providence, Rhode Island: Jamestown Publishers, 1984]).

Chapter 4: Sounds Abound concentrates on phonetic skills. The games here help children master basic decoding rules, blend sounds, isolate the sounds in single words, break words into component parts, rhyme, and use linguistic analysis.

Chapter 5: Reading and Meaning is devoted to developing reading comprehension skills. One game functions as a playful lesson in cloze procedure. Another helps children read expressively. There's a game that helps children develop story grammar, and two games that help develop vocabulary.

Chapter 6: The Writer's Trade covers writing. The five activities here are compatible with classrooms using writing process as well as any other techniques to make writing an important feature of the language-arts curriculum.

Part Three: Counting on Math

There are four chapters that cover mathematics in *Games for Learning*. The National Council of Teachers in Mathematics has developed curriculum and evaluation standards for school mathematics programs from kindergarten through grade twelve. The council's emphasis is on problem-solving, making mathematics meaningful by using manipulative materials, and finding real-life applications for mathematical ideas. The games in Part Three are designed in accord with these emphases.

Chapter 7: Counting and Beyond focuses on numeration from counting to place value. Research shows us that children learn to count in three stages. The first and easiest stage is rote counting. Rote counting is the ability to say number words in correct order. Stage two is rational counting. At this stage children can say the numbers in order and use this verbal string to accurately quantify objects. They recognize a one-to-one correspondence between numbers said and objects counted. They know that the order in which you count objects won't change the numerical outcome. They appreciate the cardinality principle—the last number you say quantifies the entire group. The third counting stage is conservation of number. Children who conserve number understand that you cannot change the count of five objects just by moving the objects around. These children are not swayed by the physical appearance of objects. They know that number, and number alone, determines how many. In general, children reach this stage sometime between the ages of five and seven. Many first-graders, therefore, do not conserve number.

How does this affect your work in the classroom? One very interesting study evaluated how a group of one hundred first-graders understood addition. These children were given the problem 2 + 3. Ninety-nine of the children answered correctly. Then the tester set out two plates with candies. On one plate he made a single pile of five candies. On the other plate he placed a pile of three candies next to a pile of two candies. Then he asked the children if they wanted the plate with the single pile of candies, the plate with the two piles, or didn't it matter? Only fifty-four out of the hundred children realized that it didn't make any difference. That meant that nearly half these first-graders could solve 2 + 3 but couldn't apply their knowledge to candy on a plate. Just as children can be fooled by the appearance of candies, adults can be fooled into thinking that children understand numbers better than they really do.

Eventually, children learn that the numbers they count are part of a system. They learn that two major concepts underlie our system—place value and base ten. These concepts are difficult. But unless youngsters come to understand them, they'll likely have problems throughout their mathematical careers.

Chapter 7 has seven games designed to help children develop skills in counting. Another four games lead children to appreciate the base ten and place value root of our number system. These games are not intended to help children with symbolic notation of numbers. Instead the games give children concrete numerical experiences that are essential to mathematical development.

Chapter 8: Addition and Subtraction is filled with games that help children master these two mathematical operations. Some of the games can, and should, be played with beans, coins, paper clips, or other concrete objects in hand. The bulk of the games here give children a way to practice and memorize number facts in a playful way. Some games help children develop skill in mental calculation. One game makes story problems fun. A couple of games help children with multidigit calculations. Your class will be eager to play games as a break from worksheets.

In *Chapter 9: Size and Shape*, you'll find games that help children recognize basic shapes and appreciate the special attributes of each shape. You'll also find games that get children happily measuring length and capacity using both English and metric scales.

Chapter 10: Multiplication and Division has games designed to give youngsters a meaningful start in multiplication and division. Three addition and subtraction games from Chapter 8 are restructured to help children master multiplication and division facts.

A final mathematical note: I've used the word *number* rather than *numeral* throughout the book. Mathematicians and teachers sometimes stress the difference between these two words. But for the sake of simplicity, I've used *number* to signify both.

Part Four: Other Subjects

There are two chapters in this section. *Chapter 11* concerns science, *Chapter 12* social studies. Playing these games serves a dual purpose. First, children will learn any number of scientific and historical facts. Primary-age children love having lots of information at their fingertips. Finding out that youngsters in colonial days waited on their parents at mealtime (as might come up in a game of TO TELL THE TRUTH) or knowing what happens when you mix baking soda and vinegar (while doing FAST AND FANTASTIC experiments) is terrific information to command.

Second, and perhaps more important, the games are designed to foster an intellectual state of mind. The scientific experiments and explorations are means to get children asking and wondering about their physical world.

A different kind of wonder is fostered in the social studies activities. Making a time capsule helps children wonder about the future. Writing letters to government officials helps children ask questions about our society today. Learning to write in hieroglyphics leads children to ponder the past. All of the activities in this section are easy to adapt to the classroom, and easy to give to your classroom parents to try out at home.

Teachers who would like more reading or math games may want to look up two other books of mine, *Games for Reading* and *Games for Math*. There are also other excellent sources of games, activities, and information for teachers. Here is a list of magazines and organizations you may find useful.

Organizations

International Reading Association, 800 Barksdale Road, P.O. Box 8139, Newark, DE   19714-8139

National Council of Teachers of English, 1111 Kenyon Road, Urbana, IL   61801

National Council of Teachers of Mathematics, 1906 Association Drive, Reston, VA   22091

National Association for the Education of Young Children, 1834 Connecticut Avenue NW, Washington, DC   20009-5786

Association for Childhood Education International, 11141 Georgia Avenue, Suite 200, Wheaton, MD   20902

Magazines

Teaching K–8, P.O. Box 54808, Boulder, CO   80322-4808

Learning, P.O. Box 2580, Boulder, CO   80322

Creative Classroom Magazine, P.O. Box 53148, Boulder, CO   80322-3148

Instructor, P.O. Box 3018, Southeastern, PA   18398

Teacher Magazine, Editorial Projects in Education, 4301 Connecticut Avenue NW, Washington, DC   20008

The Harvard Education Letter, 79 Garden Street, Cambridge, MA   02138-1423

Day Care and Early Childhood Education, Human Sciences Press, 233 Spring Street, New York, NY   10013

Math Solution, Marilyn Burns Education Associates, 150 Gate 5 Road, Suite 101, Sausalito, CA   94965

The Elementary Mathematician, Consortium for Mathematics and Its Application, 60 Lowell Street, Arlington, MA   02174